D1274828

AFTER 1989

ST ANTONY'S SERIES
General Editor: Alex Pravda, Fellow of St Antony's College, Oxford

Recent titles include:

Craig Brandist
CARNIVAL CULTURE AND THE SOVIET MODERNIST NOVEL

Jane Ellis
THE RUSSIAN ORTHODOX CHURCH

Y Hakan Erdem
SLAVERY IN THE OTTOMAN EMPIRE AND ITS DEMISE, 1800–1909

Dae Hwan Kim and Tat Yan Kong (editors)
THE KOREAN PENINSULA IN TRANSITION

Jill Krause and Neil Renwick (editors)
IDENTITIES IN INTERNATIONAL RELATIONS

Jaroslav Krejčí and Pavel Machonin
CZECHOSLOVAKIA 1918–92

Iftikhar H. Malik
STATE AND SOCIETY IN PAKISTAN

Barbara Marshall
WILLY BRANDT

Javier Martínez-Lara
BUILDING DEMOCRACY IN BRAZIL

Joseph Nevo
KING ABDALLAH AND PALESTINE

William J. Tompson
KHRUSHCHEV

After 1989

Morals, Revolution and Civil Society

Ralf Dahrendorf

St. Martin's Press
New York

in association with
ST ANTONY'S COLLEGE, OXFORD

St. Martin's Press, Scholarly and Reference Division,
175 Fifth Avenue, New York, N.Y. 10010

First published in the United States of America in 1997

This book is printed on paper suitable for recycling and
made from fully managed and sustained forest sources.

Printed in Great Britain

ISBN 0–312–17613–9

Library of Congress Cataloging-in-Publication Data
Dahrendorf, Ralf.
After 1989 : morals, revolution, and civil society / Ralf
Dahrendorf.
p.   cm. — (St. Antony's series)
Includes index.
ISBN 0–312–17613–9 (cloth)
1. World politics—1989–   2. Post-communism.   3. Political
science.   4. Civil society.   5. Europe, Eastern—Politics and
government—1989–   6. Europe, Eastern—Social conditions—1989–
7. Communism.   8. Europe—Politics and government—1989–   9. Social
sciences.   I. Title.   II. Series.
D860.D34 1997
909.82'9—dc21   97–3225
                                                              CIP

Contents

Preface

1989 was as important a date as 1945; it was a watershed. Really existing socialism collapsed, and the fatality enabled the world to discover diversity and difference in freedom. We no longer have to deal with 'systems', not even with capitalism or democracy as models of which there is only one variety, but with numerous attempts to work out ways to enhance people's life chances. What a time to be alive! The texts gathered in this volume are inspired by such sentiments. This is a book of hope both about the real world and our ability to understand it.

The subjects of the texts assembled here range widely, though 'After 1989' is their starting point and recurrent theme. The subtitle, 'Morals, Revolution and Civil Society' indicates the intention as much as the content of the volume. The future of the new democracies of East Central Europe is one of its subjects, and the wider issues of what a good society might look like, another. How do we know about such trends and objectives? This is a big question, which of necessity leads into an examination of the uses of politics, economics, history, and social science generally. And then, inevitably, there are the applications to my favourite countries, Britain and Germany, and the Europe – even the EUrope – to which they both belong.

In some ways, this book will undoubtedly fall where it should: between all stools. It is neither a book of social science nor one of politics, but both. It is neither a work of scholarship nor a popular tract, but both. It is moreover the book of a German Briton, an active intellectual, a straddler of the borders of all worlds in which he had the good fortune to be made welcome. Perhaps, lectures are the best art form to convey the flavour of such varieties of not belonging. They also serve as an excuse for the somewhat personal, even autobiographical tone – and the frequent use of the forbidden *I*-word – in the text. I have kept the style unchanged, all the way to topical allusions and references overtaken by later events because it seemed an exercise in sterility to remove them.

In one respect however this volume is firmly based. It not only appears in a distinguished series which links Oxford's St Antony's College with the publishing house of Macmillan's (and notably with the splendid editor, Tim Farmiloe), but the lectures assembled here were all given while I was Warden of St Antony's. The College is the world in a nutshell. It is so small with its 200 graduate students and 40 Fellows, and yet one senses the presence of the whole world of united (though more often divided) nations which its historians and economists, political scientists and anthropologists study. 1989 at St Antony's was unforgettable. Travellers and visitors brought news of change every week, sometimes every day. Such news fell into place by virtue of the experiences already gathered, about Spain and Latin America for example. It raised new questions about Asia, not least Japan. It made one wonder about Africa. It even led to a little boundary dispute between the Russian and East European Centre and the Middle East Centre: after the dissolution of the Soviet Union where does Central Asia belong? In the meantime, the European Centre quietly annexed those who alas! are not yet members of the European Union.

Among many reasons to thank the College which allowed me the pleasing illusion of presiding for ten years, the St Antony's experience of 1989 is certainly not the least. But the fellowship of all its members is undoubtedly the most important. Then there is my gratitude to those who have helped me do my job, including the preparation of this collection. The Warden's Secretary, Elizabeth Stevens, with her unfailing friendliness, equanimity and competence, has kept me going; I owe her a particular debt of gratitude. As I leave St Antony's my wishes go to the College itself. *Vivat, crescat, floreat,* I am tempted to say. In fact, St Antony's does not need to grow, except perhaps in wealth, but long may it live and flourish!

January 1997   R.D.

Opening Walls

1 Must Revolutions Fail?

George Orwell Lecture, given at Birkbeck College, University of London, on 15 November 1990

It is November 1990. A year ago, high winds of revolution swept the countries of Eastern and Southeastern Europe and blew away the all-too-familiar scene of *nomenklatura* rule. Vistas of open skies broke the low clouds of Brezhnev's world in which sullen submission and grey misery were the order of the day. But today, a year later, all is not well. The discovery that many of the old party bureaucrats are still in place and have even managed to turn their coats swiftly in order to become irreplaceable is almost the least of the worries. The leaders of the revolution who were once united in purpose have fallen out with each other; solidarity has turned into strife, the forum into an arena. Citizens who have just regained the right to vote find the exercise futile and fail to turn out in sufficient numbers to provide even a modest quorum (as in the Hungarian local elections). Economic conditions continue to deteriorate to the point where the *ancien régime* begins to look to many like the 'good old days'. Instead of civil society emerging triumphant, primordial tribal allegiances tempt self-appointed spokesmen to a threatening insistence on homogeneity. Generalized citizenship rights which accommodate difference and heterogeneity are the victim. Almost everywhere, there is a smell of violence in the air.

This is not, to be sure, the whole truth. People are by and large free to speak their minds. They can travel more freely. There are some signs of new economic opportunities. Journals and foundations, secular and religious organizations, small enterprises and political parties, local government and other elements of civil society are emerging. Moreover, the countries of East Central and Southeastern Europe, let alone those within the old Soviet Union, are all different. Indeed, one of the great gains of the dissolution of the Soviet bloc lies is the fact that such differences have become visible and legitimate. It is thus clearly far too early to pronounce with any degree of certainty on whether the revolution of 1989 has succeeded or not. Yet one must be allowed to wonder whether the morning after might not turn out to be as depressing in Europe's new democracies as it was in France in the 1790s, and wherever a revolution was allowed to complete its course since. For everywhere, in France and in Russia, more recently in Cuba and in Nicaragua, in several other Latin American countries, in China, two consequences of revolution have invariably occurred: traces of political democracy were

3

soon swept away by new dictatorships, and economic conditions worsened and remained bad for decades. Revolutions, it appears, create as many problems as they solve, if not more. Why? Are there reasons in the revolutionary process itself which make this outcome inevitable, or at least highly probable?

Some may wonder whether it is appropriate to call the East European events of 1989, revolutions. Certainly, Timothy Garton Ash had a point for Poland, and perhaps for Hungary, when he coined the term, *refolution*: the changes were profound, but they took the form of drastic reforms from above rather than successful pressure for change from below. In Poland, the weaknesses of gradualism are today one of the main issues dividing Tadeusz Mazowiecki and his opponent in the presidential elections, Lech Walesa. In Hungary, *refolution* in the end turned almost into revolution, though this is much more clearly the appropriate description of the events in East Germany, Czechoslovakia and Romania. In all these cases, at least the top layer of those in power was replaced rapidly and thoroughly and with their replacement went the total delegitimation of the old regime. To take one classical index of revolutions: yesterday's high treason became today's official creed, and vice versa. The law tells the story, and East Germany provides a dramatic example: the lawyers of the old GDR are not only almost all tainted, but their knowledge, for what it was worth, is now totally useless. The same is true for economic experts, for many teachers, for administrators. Watching it day by day, we may not have fully taken in just how drastic the changes were in every one of the new democracies. As political regimes, today's Czechoslovakia and Hungary, to a large extent Poland, and in varying degrees other countries, have little in common with their predecessors which were in place, say, two years ago. They are today the result of what can only be called, revolutions.

It is perhaps worth adding that violence is not a necessary ingredient of revolutions, at least in their early stages. Particularly sinister representatives of the old regime, like Romania's *conducator* Ceaucescu – or the tsar, or even the governor of the Bastille – may be killed, but by and large the first stage of revolution is one of large-scale demonstrations, of the triumphant removal of hated symbols, the occupation of public places by the people, the visible act of stripping old leaders of the paraphernalia of office, but not of killings, terror or civil war. Some of the old rulers may even be allowed to stay on, as Citizen King, as President of the Republic. Violence comes later, first as the breakdown of law and order when anomy sets in, and then as the deliberate weapon of those who try to establish themselves as new powers when the chaos is greatest, that is as terror from above, guillotine and all.

It is debatable whether every revolution has to go through all the stages which Crane Brinton regarded as a part of their 'anatomy': 'the rule of the moderates', 'the accession of the extremists', the 'reigns of terror and virtue', and eventually, 'Thermidor'. For the sake of our European neighbours, one must hope that the answer can be no, and that there are alternative ways forward. But I shall try to show presently that certain features of the revolutionary process make it very difficult to stop its slide into extremism and terror.

So far, I have defined revolutions in almost purely formal terms, as a rapid circulation of elites accompanied by a radical transformation of regimes. In terms of the question with which I am here concerned, this allows one important conclusion. Insofar as the objective of revolution is the removal of an old regime, complete revolutions do not fail. They succeed almost by definition. Nor is the clause introduced by the adjective, complete, intended as an escape hatch. Sometimes, revolutions are stopped by brutal force, generally from outside, before the old regime has been irretrievably destroyed. Perhaps, Hungary in 1956 and Czechoslovakia in 1968 can be described in these terms. The old regime survives, though even then it will never be quite the same again. The revolution of 1989, however, was complete. The old *nomenklatura* regime is not only gone, it is gone for good. Nobody will be able to retrieve or revive it. Whatever happens next – and this includes Romania – will be different from what was there before. Once old regimes crumble under the onslaught of revolutionary pressures, they are history, no more. Some might add, no less, either. History is always nemesis as well. The ghost of the *ancien régime* lingers on, for years, for decades. Are there still odd traces of it in France after 200 years? But as a regime, it has had its day. In this regard, the revolution of 1989 has succeeded, like few others before it.

Yet the formal aspect of revolutions is only one part of the story, and for the participants the least significant. They not only want to destroy a hated regime, but build a new world. What kind of new world? There are many authors to whom one could turn for the answer. The last 200 years abound with enthusiasts of revolution. Given the occasion I turned to George Orwell who was not an enthusiast but one who, in Lionel Trilling's words, 'told the truth, and told it in an exemplary way, quietly, simply, with due warning to the reader that it was only one man's truth'. I reread *Homage to Catalonia*. Soon after his arrival in Spain, Orwell noted: 'Nobody said "Señor" or "Don" or even "Usted"; everyone called everyone else "Comrade" and "Thou", and said "Salud!" instead of "Buenos dias".' However, if that was a part of the revolution, the process had not gone much further. Worse, 'in reality it was the Communists above all others who prevented revolution in

Spain'. Only the Anarchists insisted on basic equality, local power, workers' councils, common ownership. 'The Communists' emphasis is always on centralism and efficiency, the Anarchists' on liberty and equality.' The Communists demanded attention to the war first and revolution later, and thereby played into the hands of the Fascists; the Anarchists wanted democracy now, but they did not prevail.

Democracy. No other word sums up better the dreams of revolutionaries in Europe and elsewhere in the last 200 years. 'We the people' are both the subject and the theme of revolutions. Timothy Garton Ash, like Orwell committed without being sentimental, and intent above all on telling the truth, tells us that 'the leaders of the revolutions or refolutions had a startlingly clear idea of the constitutional order they wanted to build' which 'bore not a little resemblance' to that of the American revolution. He also invokes the concept of civil society as a revolutionary dream. 'There should be forms of association, national, regional, local, professional, which would be voluntary, authentic, democratic.' And, as the motto of his book *We the People*, Garton Ash uses the words from President Vaclav Havel's 1990 New Year's Address: 'People, your government has returned to you!'

Well said, but can governments ever fulfil this promise? Democracy has two quite different kinds of meaning. One is constitutional, an arrangement by which it is possible to remove governments without revolution, by elections, parliaments and the rest. The other meaning of democracy is much more fundamental. Both Orwell and Garton Ash hint at it in engagingly practical terms by talking about workers' councils and professional organizations. But other ideas creep into their reports. Democracy must be authentic; government must return to the people; equality must become real. There is the Rousseauean dream of a *volonté générale* which has inspired the revolutionaries of France in 1789, a general will which mysteriously leads all to agree without force or constraint. Marx has developed the concept in his rare and reluctant hints at the world after the final revolution which would be a world of association rather than domination, and thus of equality rather than class. The idea lives on to the present day, as in Jürgen Habermas's yearning for a society of 'unconstrained communication', of consensus by voluntary and permanent discourse between equals.

The idea is engaging, even thrilling. It is a vision of hope which lifts people's spirits above the routine of normalcy. After all, everyday life in society is both boring and annoying. It is the never-ending roleplay of people who behave by and large in accordance with expectations which they have not invented and cannot change. Moreover, the theatre in which this roleplay takes place clearly has directors somewhere, judging from the fact that one cannot break rules without paying a price. Society is constrained by norms and sanctions and by those who enforce and impose them. Sometimes, though comparatively rarely, the routine is broken. Not just Catholic countries know a carnival season in which everything is turned upside down by people in masks and fancy dress, and the official society is suspended, though the fun usually ends in a long and often arduous fast of lent. Strikes are a nuisance to employers and nowadays to customers as well, but for those involved they are often a welcome break in the monotony of life. Crime is more than a nuisance, yet it sells millions of copies of newspapers with lurid accounts to law-abiding readers who seem to relish the vicarious excitement of seeing normal expectations flouted.

The most dramatic suspension of everyday life is probably war. In wars, even taboos are explicitly, indeed officially, broken. People are encouraged to kill. Children are told to leave their parents. Husbands and wives are separated as a matter of public policy. Many ordinary activities are stopped. But, of course, as in carnivals and strikes the permission to do the impermissible is itself highly regulated. War is to the political right what revolutions are to the left: the suspension of normal society. In both cases, private lives and public events merge into one, history becomes individual biography and vice versa. Both lay bare the raw bones of life underneath all the skin and the fat of civil and bourgeois society. But whereas war is in principle highly controlled, revolutions are in principle open-ended. This has to do with the fact that wars confirm the powers that be, or are intended to do so, whereas revolutions remove them. In practice, the two are often not that far apart, as George Orwell found. Not surprisingly, the Communists with their interest in 'centralism and efficiency' cared more about war than revolution. For the two call upon very different human emotions and values. War is often about domination and always about self-assertion, whereas revolution is about hope.

It is hope for a totally different world. Its features are described with varying degrees of sophistication and of emotion. They range from anarchy in the strict sense to an equally strict concept of association. Whatever the description, the common denominator of revolutionary hopes is a society (if that is still the word) in which all are equal and no one has power over others, a co-operative society, a giant college. 'The place of the old bourgeois society with its classes and class conflicts is taken by an association in which the free development of everyone is the condition of the free development of all.'

Thus Marx and Engels in a familiar phrase which defines the objective of the proletariat in its 'battle for democracy'. But democracy in this sense cannot be. There may have been some 'tribes without rulers' (though one must be allowed to wonder about unconfirmed reports by anthropologists), and there are oligarchic associations like Oxford colleges in which unconstrained discourse fills the High Table nights – but real human societies are about norms, and norms require sanctions which in turn need sanctioning agencies and thus structures of authority. Perhaps it is wrong to rule out altogether the dream of anarchy – the unheard-of may happen after all – but so far as we know the social contract of association has invariably included a contract of domination. Where people set rules by which they live, some are more equal than others.

The revolutionary dream of a government which has returned to the people must therefore fail. In 1990, its failure is there for everyone to see. The tender revolutionaries of East Germany's New Forum and related groups still cannot understand how they failed to get more than 3 per cent of the popular vote in the first free elections on 18 March, but the electorate was perhaps shrewder than the churchmen who led the demonstrations of Leipzig on those memorable Mondays last autumn. Like Solidarnosc in Poland, the Civic Forum in Czechoslovakia is ending in tears. The return of government to the people means no government at all; 'the people' are unable to initiate change beyond the destructive moments of revolution. Could it be that 'people power' is invariably negative, the power to remove rather than to move? In any case, fundamental democracy is an error, and a costly error at that.

It is an error incidentally which Lenin never committed. 'We are not Utopians,' he said in *State and Revolution*. 'We are not "dreaming" of suddenly being able to manage without administration or subordination ... We will carry out the socialist revolution with people as they are, people who cannot live without subordination, without control, without "supervisors and bookkeepers".' And so the dictatorship of the proletariat took its course, more and more dictatorship with less and less involvement of the proletariat, or any other major social group for that matter. More often than not the dream of pure association ends in pure domination. The question is how to domesticate power, not how to remove it.

This is the question of the other, the constitutional concept of democracy, and it raises the most serious issue of all. Let me recapitulate the argument so far. Revolutions, including the revolution of 1989, succeed in destroying the old regime for good. Revolutions fail to create a totally different world of fundamental democracy. In that sense they are bound to disappoint the extravagant hopes to which they gave birth. But what about the institutions of open societies which regulate conflict and allow of change without violence?

I have talked so far as if revolutions are isolated events, like natural catastrophes, arriving from nowhere and leaving behind a scene of destruction and disappointment. Many of those who pinned their hopes for a totally different world on revolutions would have used voluntaristic rather than catastrophic images but had, in fact, the same mistaken belief. They thought that revolutions could be made, organized, created at will, that it took no more than a few determined revolutionaries to bring about change. They should have read their Marx – as well as other more recent authors – better.

Revolutionary situations are rare and serious conditions of human affairs. They occur when a ruling class has held down not just other groups but also an existing potential for change for extended periods of time. The point about the Brezhnevian *nomenklatura* was on the one hand an entrenched system of privilege backed up by brute force as well as by devious control through a state security apparatus. But it was on the other hand the visible progress of non-communist countries almost next door. In other words, the *nomenklatura* not only held down all other groups, but also held back opportunities which were there for everyone to see. It would not be altogether inappropriate to use Marxian language and say that a class conflict was fuelled by the inability of prevailing conditions ('relations of production') to accommodate a potential for improvement ('forces of production'). The deception of official statistics no longer worked; indeed the entire system of ideological deception began to fall apart. Those who were not beneficiaries of the system saw only two possibilities: to leave or to remove the system. East Germans did both; others with less choice had to concentrate on political change.

Revolutionary situations are not revolutions. They are a powderkeg but someone has to set it alight. More precisely, an element of hope has to be thrown into a revolutionary situation to make it explode. This is usually provided by some indication of the weakness of the ruling class, a reform which encourages people to push further, a sign of insecurity which destroys the pretence. Ceaucescu's face when during his address to a crowd he realized that his 'supporters' were actually his enemies is an example, as is the confusion of decisions surrounding the opening of the Berlin Wall. The deeper source of the spark of hope in the events of 1989 was undoubtedly President Gorbachev and his evident decision not to intervene if and when people chose to do it their way.

So the process began, with all the euphoria of the extraordinary which is still so vivid in our memories. For weeks, many people went on huge demonstrations instead of going to work. (East Germans, I believe, did both.) Suddenly the seemingly immovable structures of *nomenklatura* rule gave way. Reform Communists took over from traditionalists, only to be removed themselves within a matter of days. The monopoly of the Communist Party collapsed first at the top and then, though much more slowly, at every level. Elections were planned, campaigns started. In some countries, like Bulgaria, a new elected government came in so quickly that the forces of change had barely had the time to organize. With the exception of Romania, all looked well at some point between the inauguration of Vaclav Havel at the end of December 1989 and, say, Easter 1990.

However, several complications occurred during that process and since. I have described them in some detail in my *Reflections on the Revolution in Europe*, so that the briefest of summaries must suffice here. One is the collapse of the centre. Once the Party was removed from its monopoly position, the state machinery had become fragile if not hollow. What this means is now demonstrated in an extreme fashion by the Soviet Union, where the President can issue any number of decrees which have virtually no effect on what happens on the ground. In the absence of a functioning administration the decrees remain paper, waste paper. In the case of East Germany, the takeover by West Germany has concealed the extent to which the elected government had lost, or perhaps never gained, authority. Hungary and Czechoslovakia, to say nothing of Yugoslavia, Romania, Bulgaria, do not have this opportunity. In all these countries the question is not so much whether the government is doing the right things or not, but whether it is capable of doing anything at all. The *refolution* of Poland has saved the country from such a fate so far, but President Walesa may well feel tempted to take measures which destroy what is left of the state apparatus.

To the collapse of the centre must be added the economic valley of tears. This is painful at the best of times, as the Polish, or indeed the East German example shows. It is unbearable if it is coupled with the near-total absence of central authorities, as in the old Soviet Union. It leads to disenchantment in Hungary, Czechoslovakia and other countries in between the extremes. The risk is high that people conclude that democracy means high prices, high unemployment, low incomes for most and speculative profits for a few. Why vote if this is the result? Indeed why have democracy at all?

Then there is the re-emergence of the tribe, of primordial ties and emotions. Communism was among other things a homogenizing – some would say, a modernizing – force. Now that it is gone, older national and religious ligatures come to the fore. Since people have little to hold on to, and even less to eat, they fall for prophets who fill their minds and hearts with the hatred of others in the name of self-determination.

It is possible to map a road from communism to freedom, from *nomenklatura* rule to the institutions of democracy. Nor is such a map merely that of a fantasy world which never was. The American revolution probably does not deserve this name, but it is a great example of the deliberate creation of a constitution of liberty. The *Federalist Papers* contain much that is relevant to the countries of East Central Europe. More recently, there is the success story of West Germany after the war which is relevant because of its central feature, the simultaneous need for political and economic reform. This comparison too is obviously inappropriate in a number of respects, though it shows that it is possible to build an open society amidst the debris of tyranny.

The problem is one of nerve, of luck and of a clear sense of direction. Political institutions are quickly set up, though it takes much longer to anchor them in people's minds and hearts. What Samuel Huntington has called the 'two-turnover test' probably has to be applied before they are safe; that is two changes of government by democratic means have to happen. The rule of law raises its own difficult issues, especially in countries which have inherited a corrupt system of party rule; but the necessary conditions can be spelt out. Economic reform towards a market-based order takes longer. It is, as we see only too clearly in 1990, technically difficult. Privatization alone raises a number of initially almost insuperable problems. Techniques of change apart, economic reform leads of necessity through the valley of tears of which I have spoken. Prices rise, wages fall, unemployment spreads before any programme of change begins to grip. Four years is a short period for an economy to pass through the worst and slowly begin the upward climb. Yet it can be done. Both political and economic reform will however have to be anchored in vibrant civil societies, and James Madison recognized clearly, in his contributions to the *Federalist*, just how difficult they are to bring about. If the new Germany can build on a reliable and firm democratic tradition which extends beyond political institutions and economic success, this will be the most significant achievement of West German developments since the war. Once again, the example shows that it can be done.

But will it be done? The collapse of the centre, the depth of the economic valley of tears and the return of primordial forces which work against a society of accepted diversity and regulated conflict, must raise serious doubts. None of these applied to the establishment of the United States of America, unless one wants to regard the theme of the *Federalist* itself, the creation of an effective centre, as an equivalent problem. In postwar Germany, economic conditions were so bad at the outset that the valley of tears seemed bearable, or at any rate inescapable, to most. Closer to my theme in this lecture, the story of the French Revolution does not hold out much hope. Curiously, 1789 sent a message of democracy in the institutional sense to countries which had not experienced a revolution, but in France, the early seeds of democracy perished in the 'reign of terror and virtue', and it took decades for their remnants to grow and bear fruit. Even economically, what evidence we have of economic activity and notably trade, shows that it took France three decades to return to the pre-revolutionary state of affairs.

Before I take this argument to what must now seem its inevitable conclusion, let me make one point loud and clear. Social theories do not constitute or reflect historical necessities. The story of revolution has a certain inner logic. This is notably the case where an old regime has been dislodged which held a monopoly in political as well as economic and virtually all other respects. The post-revolutionary situation is one of near-anomy in which disenchantment is almost unavoidable. Such disenchantment does not create a very favourable climate for the establishment of lasting democratic institutions. It is even likely to encourage radical minorities or individuals to seek power in the name of objectives and with methods which are anything but democratic. But none of this is bound to happen.

For one thing, our theories may be wrong. I confess to a new version of Karl Popper's insistence on falsification as the instrument of discovering the truth, in that I hope nothing as much in this year 1990 as that our current theories of revolution turn out to be wrong, and that the countries of East Central Europe will find a path towards the open society. For another thing, general theories by their very nature fail to take account of particular and often unique conditions in given societies. For want of a better word, we often call such conditions, cultural. Hungary is a country in which, rather like in Italy, the economic macro-picture will probably always look bad, or at least problematic, while in real life, real people somehow find a way to make do, and more. Poland's sense of national destiny has seen the country through many a crisis, and we may yet find that an institutional practice develops which, while far from textbook notions of democracy, is nevertheless a kind of free society. The imagination of reality is forever greater than that of theory, sometimes for worse, but often for better. There is hope.

There is also an environment which is on the whole favourable to the progress of the constitution of liberty. East Germany enjoyed the unique opportunity of integration into a democratic united Germany. A democratic united Europe is as yet less real and relevant, and certainly much less generous. Still, the fortunate Europe to which we belong, exists and has a certain magnetic effect even if it does not discharge its evident responsibilities very impressively.

But when all this is said and done, the main conclusion remains. The revolution of 1989, like other revolutions before it, has succeeded in removing an old regime which will not return. The revolution of 1989, like other revolutions before it, was bound to disappoint those who entered it with extravagant hopes for a new world of unconstrained discourse, equality and fundamental democracy. Many may find these two consequences a cause for delight, and at any rate not one for great concern. But like other revolutions before it, the revolution of 1989 also makes the road to freedom extremely hazardous. It has created conditions which militate against successful political reform, effective economic reform and the firm establishment of civil societies. Countries may overcome the obstacles, but the plain fact remains that revolutions are simply not very helpful when it comes to the constitution of liberty. This may not be a terribly useful remark, since revolutions happen once conditions have deteriorated to the point of a revolutionary situation. Yet it reminds us of the need for strategic change at the right time, and thus for institutions which make it possible without upheaval, let alone violence, to change course and even to change governments. Revolutions must fail, and it is therefore the first requirement of the constitution of liberty to make sure that they need not happen.

2 The Open Society and Its Fears

Keynote Address to the 25th German Sociological Congress in Frankfurt/Main, 12 October 1990

On re-reading the *Transactions* of the agitated Sixteenth German Sociological Congress in April 1968 here in Frankfurt, I was struck by the episode at the end of the debate on the paper entitled 'Power, Class Relations, and Stratification'. One of the authors of the collective product (which made me visibly angry at the time) ended his final contribution to the debate with the declaration: 'In the name of the collaborators of our paper I hereby inform the participants of the Sixteenth German Sociological Congress that we shall pass on the honorarium for the jointly presented paper to the collection arranged by the Socialist Student Society in favour of deserters from the American army. We invite Mr Dahrendorf as well as the other recipients of honoraria to do the same.' The applause was tremendous. That was predictable at the time, but how times have changed! No one has offered me an honorarium for today's lecture. Perhaps I should, on the contrary, have paid for the favour, like the authors of the *Transactions* of the National Academy of Sciences in the United States whose first footnote always says 'This is an advertisement', because they have paid a subsidy for the publication.

In 1968, Heinrich Popitz chaired the discussion, and with his endearing unaggressive contrariness he stated at the end of the debate that he thought the objective of the socialist honorarium was fine, but he totally disagreed with the 'invitation to all others to do the same. I regard that as repression. I respond to it by my decision to give my honorarium to the association of Roman Catholic charities.'

In the run-up to the Frankfurt Sociological Congress of that fateful year 1968 there had been lively discussions within the Committee of the Sociological Association about its theme: 'Late Capitalism or Industrial Society?' Today, when both have gone down the river and very different themes dominate debate, this sounds almost touching. At the time it separated those who believed in the inevitable, and at any rate the desirable, end of the Western social system, from those who were prepared to seek reforms of industrial societies. To us, the participants, the confrontation seemed important. It continued into methodological antagonisms (which had become fashionable since the 'positivism dispute' in the early sixties), led to widely

14

divergent notions of the relation between theory and practice, and it reflected the hopes which guide all images of society, including that of the open society. Insofar as the Frankfurt School was more than a youth cult which either includes or excludes but will not tolerate questions, its main effect was to suggest the image of a totally different world without seriously questioning the pleasures, indeed luxuries, of the real world. Late capitalism had always *inter alia* been a world of subtle delights, of sublime decadence, whereas industrial society was driven by harder, less comfortable preferences such as class interests. 'Class?' I shall never forget the reaction by Max Horkheimer and Theodor Adorno to my wish to work on the subject when I was their young assistant: 'Is it really necessary to talk about class?' This was in 1954; Adenauer had just been re-elected with an enhanced majority. Thus I left the Institute and took my senior doctorate on 'Class and Class Conflict in Industrial Society' at the University of the Saar which was then still tinged by the predilections of its French founders.

All this was a long time ago. The 68ers have, so to speak, grown up, and a little old as well. Today, the alternative, 'late capitalism or industrial society', no longer makes much sense. At any rate the other alternative of open and closed societies is more topical, especially if one wishes to return to the subject of the 1968 debate, 'Power, Class Relations, and Stratification'. Late capitalist industrial societies have proven amazingly capable of reform or at least change. One could have known this: John Maynard Keynes and William Beveridge, the inventors of a modern economic policy of controlled money supply and demand management, and of a welfare state without Bismarckian paternalism but as an instrument of citizenship rights for all, had already made their mark. Still, it was in the last quarter-century that their influence became sustained. The fact that the OECD societies today are given so many names, postindustrial and risk-prone, anomic and perhaps even classless, only serves to demonstrate the embarrassment of applying to it old, yet still important categories like power and class.

On the other hand, these theories fit the closed societies of our time well; they did in particular apply to the now crumbling countries of *nomenklatura* socialism. These were and are still industrial societies. At least until the revolution of 1989 they had ruling and suppressed classes. They were incapable of gradual reform. They became increasingly rigid, especially in the Brezhnev era. Classical sociological theory could have told us that such trends would have a sorry, or rather a revolutionary ending. Closed societies do not last. They nevertheless exercise a fatal attraction for people who cannot bear the strains of liberty. The following remarks will deal with these issues and with the great social alternatives of our time.

The distinction between open and closed societies is even more important than Karl Popper thought. It also requires conceptual precision. Familiar notions can help in this process. The difference between monopolistic and pluralistic structures makes good sense, as does that between market and plan. Equally, Popper's insistence that open societies harbour institutions which make it possible to remove governments without bloodshed, has important implications. In open societies it is neither one single position or agency nor a detailed guidebook which brings about the co-ordination of many actors. Even the rules set in the name of the monopoly of violence embodied in the state define only boundaries of behaviour and leave a wide range of options open within. In practice it is not always easy to distinguish formal and substantive rules; even rules of the game have a fatal tendency to benefit one side more than the other; however in this context it is sufficient to indicate intentions. In open societies everything is allowed which is not explicitly forbidden. Moreover, as little as possible is forbidden, and what is allowed is left to individual choice. Role expectations are permissive rather than prescriptive in nature. Roles themselves are throughout achievable and not ascribed. Open societies favour unconstrained change.

Such statements are full of pitfalls. Does not even the most open society in this sense include important elements of closure, and vice versa? For example, what about the monopoly of violence of the state? Here, concepts are useful which allow precise definition. 'Option' is such a concept. Open societies increase, closed societies reduce options. Among options there is one which might well provide a helpful index, that is mobility. Open societies demand, closed societies restrict mobility. I am using this term in its widest sense: for geographical migration and for social movements up and down the scale, but also for the behaviour of floating voters and for the mobility of economic factors of production. The 'four freedoms' of the single-market project of the European Community (freedom to exchange goods, services, to move capital and to use the labour market) promote mobility. Quite generally we tend in everyday language to equate freedom with mobility, and there are often good reasons for everyday language.

This raises familiar and not-so-familiar questions of political theory. At what point does openness turn into anarchy, indeed anomy? (Those in the know will not be surprised that there is hidden in every advocate of the open society a secret anarch, if not anarchist.) How much closure is a condition of the very possibility of society, and thereby of progress and real freedom? To put it in Hayek's language which is apposite here: how can the 'constitution of liberty' be determined? But equally the other way round, and with Adam Smith for whom three businessmen who have a friendly meeting called forth concerns about the invisible hand: is there possibly a tendency intrinsic to all societies to form if not monopolies then at least cartels? How much better than *nomenklatura* socialism is bureaucratic corporatism? How much power in which constellations does a free society require, and how much does it permit?

I hint at such questions with extreme, almost impermissible brevity in order to support the assertion that the concepts of the open and the closed society are neither empty shells nor hypostasized principles of political philosophy. At least they need not be such. They may give useful indications for the analysis of social changes in their sociopolitical and socioeconomic dimensions which are at issue here.

The revolution of 1989 has provided rich material for such analysis. The societies or real socialism were largely closed societies. Closed does not necessarily mean totalitarian. Conceptually (though not for the people concerned) totalitarianism is the simpler form of power. Romania provides the example. The fact that totalitarian power is focused on the person of the leader means that in order to achieve change one initially need do no more than remove the ruler. However one will then discover that the basic constellation and the temptation of monopolistic power have remained in existence. Society is missing, civil society; one finds none of the agencies and organizations which protect the individual from the grip of the rulers. A circle of violence is set in motion which it is hard to break. The Romanian experience gives cause for new questions about 20 July 1944 for example: what would have happened, if? Millions would still be alive. That alone was – and is in Romania – sufficient justification. But in 1944 too it is unlikely that an open society would have emerged immediately.

Nomenklatura rule has other features. There are in fact political, economic and even social structures, at least in form and appearance. Ministers, managers and heads of so-called 'social organizations' can be identified. Yet the word 'structure' is misleading in this context. As such the incumbents of familiar positions are merely the bricks and mortar for the construction of the state. The structure is created by the monopolistic party. If one takes the party – or even only its monopoly – away, the edifice collapses. It is as if the mortar dissolves at a signal which has held the bricks of the social edifice together. Nothing works any more. There remains the debris which here and there still betrays the traces of the building to which its elements once belonged.

The result can be frightening. The former GDR is one of the extreme cases. On 18 March 1990, when a parliament, the *Volkskammer*, was elected and a government was formed, the monopoly of the party, the SED, was already broken. There were thus no structures of power left whose incumbents could be replaced or newly chosen by elections. Parliament and government merely played a power game, if with grim though pardonable seriousness. Laws were enacted which had no effect whatsoever. Coalition crises were acted out, ministers were appointed and sacked, but the whole process remained mere theatre, state theatre with all the requisite props. The link between the alleged decision-making centre and the real field of action was missing. It is still missing. New administrative structures are built but slowly. Institutions like the *Treuhand*, created to transfer publicly owned businesses, are more important than all government departments. In this regard, as in others, only the takeover by the old Federal Republic will in due course create new – and open – structures.

Poland has tried to take a different route. It did not experience a revolution but instead what Timothy Garton Ash has called, a *refolution*, that is, reforms with revolutionary effect, introduced from above. The Round Table kept many members of the old *nomenklatura* in their old positions. It is as if the Mazowiecki–Balcerowicz–Kuron government had assumed the role of the *politburo* of old and left many communist officials as executive agents in place. This was a highly effective way forward but it also left, above and beyond the cost of economic reform, open flanks for criticism. Lech Walesa, to whom we owe so much of the new liberty, now tries to ignite the resulting disaffection because he cannot bear to remain at the Gdansk periphery of events. He probably does not fully understand what he is doing, but if he is elected President in the forthcoming election, there is a real risk that Poland will follow its neighbours into the dissolution of structures.

The Soviet Union provides the most disquietening example of this process. President Gorbachev deserves his place in history for the courage and consistency with which he has opened doors: *glasnost*, the independence of former satellite countries, in the end the liquidation of the monopoly of the Communist Party. For many observers it looked as if in this process he had amassed more and more power in his hands, until in the end the president governs largely by decrees with the help of his presidential council. But in truth this power is hollow. Gorbachev's decrees remain paper laws. Nobody executes what the president orders or even what parliament decides. Symptoms of anomy and thus of dissolution grow. Districts of the city of Moscow – no longer even the mayor's central city administration – conclude 'trade agreements' with nearby villages and supervise them closely. The larger picture is no different. The Estonians have given up on negotiations in the Kremlin and instead reach agreements partly with Finland and Sweden, partly with Petersburg. While the leaden hand of the *nomenklatura* still lies heavily on the people in many Russian communities, it is no longer linked to a nerve centre; it just lies there. Moreover thousands of nuclear and other weapons lie there too, and no one controls them effectively.

This is, as indicated, material for the main theme of my remarks. It is no accident that phenomena of mobility emerged at key points of the processes described here. One remembers the GDR holidaymakers in Hungary and in the then CSSR. Everywhere, options were demanded. The most tragic symptom of the change can be found in that personalized pure mobility, mobility in and for itself as it were, that is the millions of refugees who are now roaming through the former Soviet Union, through Europe and the world beyond. Arguably they represent the characteristic social figure of our time. Those who still have rooted structures close their eyes to the refugees. The day of German unity was also the day of the introduction of compulsory visas for Poles. In this way a dangerous new automatism is set in motion. Whoever shuts himself off to the outside, pays a price within. This is at the very least a tangible price of police authorities, registration forms and other formalities; but a mentality of closure often follows suit. The consequences are serious. The needs of the refugees and the fears of the natives are equally understandable. Here is one of those dilemmas which are not easily resolved.

It would be tempting, and in a systematic context necessary too, to link such topical observations with the classical subjects of power, class and stratification. In doing so one would extend in starker colours some of the lines of argument used in the debates of the 1968 Sociological Congress. One would then have to speak of the double diffusion of power in the open societies of the OECD world, of its distribution over a variety of centres, and of its 'division of labour' in bureaucratic structures. One would also take up the thread of the 'disparities of realms of life' which have taken the place of class structures. One would wish to ask how the new underclass of the very poor and the long-term unemployed fits into the picture. The political consequences of the process of diffusion of power would have to be looked at, notably the fact that the old parties have become mere shells for all kinds of new contents. If they had the courage of the Italian communists, they would all, at least for a while, call themselves, *la cosa*, 'the thing', no more and no less. Questions would have to be asked about new sources of power. The great productive force of transnational enterprises would have to be considered, and the fact that the relations of production of post-industrial societies (or whatever one wants to call them) are lagging far behind. One would have to examine the question of whether there is an international class struggle, or whether the remaining Third World is rather like a giant underclass, a living indictment of the values professed by those in power but without strength or power when the hegemony of the majority class is threatened. In short, it would be necessary to have another look at the modern social conflict, its transformations as well as its continuities.

However, I shall not even try to do all this here. Instead I want to supplement the topical reflections on the revolution of 1989 and deepen them on the assumption that they raise fundamental questions of society. For this at least revolutions do achieve: they remind us of the preamble and the first articles of the social contract and force us either to reaffirm or to reformulate them.

What is the motive force of the new democracies of East Central Europe? Which is the implicit or explicit direction of the changes which are happening under our eyes? It is not, or so I assert, another 'system'. The process of dissolution which I have alluded to, does not serve the purpose of replacing the old monoply by a new one, not even by Hayek's monopoly of the 'natural' sources of social morality. What is at issue is, rather, the open society. This means that the monopolistic structures of the old regime are replaced by a world of options and of mobility. This is a big step forward. The first steps towards the open society are often accompanied by euphoria; ever new experiences of success wait along the way. But the process does not answer all questions, nor does it mark the end of history. I have already pointed to the fears which accompany the path into the open society. Perhaps the open society itself has deficiencies and weaknesses which provide the structural refutation of Fukuyama's misleading image of the 'end of history'.

Among the questions which would have to be examined in a more systematic analysis there is one which makes the 'disparities of realms of life' especially evident, that is, the threats to our environment. The risk society is an inescapable subject. The link between the quality of the human habitat, the role of energy for economy and society, the habits and expectations of the majority and the peaceful symbiosis of nations, all become evident in the Gulf War but point beyond it as well. The 'responsibility principle' is obviously a good thing though it does raise the question of whether in coping with one risk we do not incur another, potentially even greater one. Just as the dictatorship of the proletariat was too high a price to pay for the dream of socialism, it may well be that the benevolent hegemony of those who claim to be able to identify all risks and above all to know how to cope with them, will in the end create a closed society in which it is no longer worth living. The dilemma exists and it bids us caution.

However, another dilemma is closer to my subject here. It has been alluded to already. I am speaking of the dilemma of anomy. This too needs to be treated with caution. Life chances are in the first instance options. These are themselves multidimensional. They have at least a supply side and a demand side. Life chances entail a wide range of choices, not just of consumer goods and material pleasures but of opportunities of mobility; a diversity of media, a plurality of parties are part and parcel of the supply of options. But options include entitlements, chances of access too. They imply that generalized civic status which is so well described by the word, citizenship. In both respects options are incomplete everywhere, and one must hope that the supply decade of the 1980s will be followed by a new entitlement decade in the 1990s.

However, even where options combine equal opportunities with a wide range of choices, life chances remain incomplete. It is not enough that everyone can do a lot of things. What is missing is the element of meaning to make sense of options; deep structures are missing, ligatures. This is a complex, even problematic concept with which sociologists have struggled without lasting success since the beginnings of the discipline. (It is often said that sociology itself originated at the break points of old deep structures and above all at the great turning point 'from status to contract', with which to some extent we are still struggling today.) It is easy to see that open societies with their mobility have a tendency to dissolve ligatures, whereas closed societies harden them into dogma and thus make them instruments of power. There is, as it were, an excess of linkages as well as an unacceptable deficiency and the dilemma has much to do with the subject of liberty.

This observation takes us back to the post-communist world. In East and Southeast Central Europe the collapse of the *nomenklatura* has left behind not just an administrative vacuum. With the *nomenklatura* an ideology has collapsed. It had been hollow for a long time, and was often mere pretence rather than an honest faith; yet it leaves behind emptiness. Klimova, the Czechoslovak authoress, is quoted with the statement: 'In the old days nothing was allowed and everything was important; nowadays everything is allowed and nothing is important any more.' There can hardly be a more striking way of putting into words the problem with which we are concerned here.

Traces of older ligatures reappear in this vacuum. Some put their feet in them firmly and deeply. Alexander Solshenizyn has found words to describe the horrors of the Gulag Archipelago which along with images of Auschwitz will remain with many of us forever. But now he extols a soul of the Russian people which the Polish intellectual Adam Michnik has rightly attacked as the ugly one of the 'two faces of Europe'. Such Slavophilia is but one version of the revival of a nationalism which regards the nation not as the political framework of the rule of law, but as the intolerant unit of belonging and of exclusion. Ukrainians and Usbeks, Slovenes and Slovaks want above all homogeneous nations, societies without ethnic and cultural and religious differences, homes for the soul not for mature citizens.

It is not hard to understand some of the motives for such desires. National independence was and is for many a necessary condition of liberty. For Hungarians there was no chance of creating an open society within the Soviet Empire, and the same may well be true for Estonians, Latvians and Lithuanians. But the necessary condition is not sufficient. The nation-state is but the framework for the open society, and not its shape and its colour. 'From entirely equals no state can emerge', Aristotle rightly said. Even civil rights get their meaning through living with difference. They embody the guaranteed basic rights of all, including the chance to pursue one's own cultural preferences. But as such they do not create ligatures. Nor do rights and linkages simply complement each other. More often civil rights have been in conflict with powerful forces of belonging, thus with the deep structures of linkages which can serve to deny the rights of others (and rights are always those of others). Here lies the deeper cause of the clashes between the two wings of Solidarnosc in Poland, or of Christian Democrats and Free Democrats in Hungary. In the dissolving states of what was Yugoslavia, or the Soviet Union for that matter, such differences are the source of future conflicts.

Beyond the search for national ligatures in the face of questions which the open society does not and cannot answer, other forces are making similar claims. They are above all religious in nature. The very word, re*lig*ion, contains the same Latin root as *lig*atures: it is about linkages which reach deeper than social relations established by contract. Fundamentalism is a generalizing concept for what is meant here though it does not mislead. The secularized societies of the 'West' (which include those of the old East though not the Orient) have either spurned religion or declared it a private affair. But the Caesar which can be separated from God in this way exists only in very few parts of the world, perhaps in the end only in the United States of America. In Islamic societies there are no secular rulers without God nor is there a God without secular significance. In this, Islam is not alone. On balance, the world humans have created for themselves is a Catholic rather than a Protestant arrangement.

As a rule, the invasion of demanding ligatures into the opportunities of the open society means violence. This may be the suppression and persecution of minorities or of dissidents. It may also turn into a holy war against unbelievers beyond the boundaries. The open society often finds itself at the losing end of such conflicts. (Is anyone persuaded by talk about creating a new order of democracy and liberty on the Persian Gulf?) It is in any case far from certain that the meaning-starved life chances of the free world will be victorious over the opportunity-starved decrees of meaning in the illiberal world.

Practical questions are not normally posed in such extreme alternatives; theoretical questions should therefore not be confined to these terms. The theme of these reflections on the fears which accompany and threaten open societies is familiar: can open societies provide meaning? What ligatures are permitted, promoted, demanded by open societies? What does the society of chances and options have to offer to the hearts of its citizens? What kindles the enthusiasm of enlightened and free human beings? And if there should be little to achieve this end: who or what protects them from the enthusiasm of others, of Ukrainian nationalists, of Islamic fundamentalists, of Solshenitzyn, of the Rembrandt German in many a guise?

I shall disappoint those among you who expect an answer from me. Ordinarily I do not find it difficult to live with the harder structures of the open society (just as the industrial society with its class structures has not led me into the temptation of Utopia). But I can see that my personal experience must not be generalized. Moreover, I appreciate the questions which Jürgen Habermas puts persistently and plausibly, especially those for a 'reasonable identity' in modern societies. In a way the formation of ligatures is his theme. He seeks a social contract which is more than a legally sanctioned piece of paper.

In this context, constitutional patriotism has its place. If one wonders where the older open societies of England and North America find their ligatures, one encounters some rarely discussed phenomena. England was dominated for a long time by a sense of being God's chosen democracy; there are still traces of that feeling. Edmund Burke put this well when he spoke of 'the primeval contract of eternal society'. This is how it is, and no great debate is needed about it. Even the supreme constitutional principle of the 'sovereignty of the Queen in Parliament' confirms this consciousness of an unbroken history. In the United States of America Tocqueville has pointed early to the great significance of the churches. They enter into a strange alliance with the constitution which makes it possible on all sorts of occasions to say 'God bless America' with the hand on one's heart and tears in one's eyes. Perhaps such traditions are today beginning to crumble even in the two old democracies, but they have managed to reconcile democratic institutions and ligatures in a remarkable manner.

Whether a German constitutional patriotism can achieve something similar remains to be seen. A lot will depend on the anchor chosen to fasten German unity. Is it precarious economic power, a cloudy national or even European dream, or the strength of a Basic Law which by now has a respectable history of success? The question is still open. It will not be answered by elections or governmental declarations. Ligatures can be created, but then they have to take root and begin to grow.

If I had been offered an honorarium for these remarks, to whom would I give the money in the light of such conclusions? In the end to Catholic charities after all? No, but perhaps to a German Civic Foundation which does not yet exist but which might be set up in order to fill the structures of the open society with the lifeblood of civil society.

3 Citizens in Search of Meaning

Address given at the Award Ceremony of the Toynbee Prize at St Antony's College, Oxford, on 20 October 1990

If a social scientist, indeed worse, one whose profession used to be sociology, receives a prize in the name of a great historian, one must be allowed to wonder. Has the social scientist abandoned his ways? Has he given up (in Windelband's clumsy but useful terms) the 'nomothetic' for the 'idiographic', the general for the particular, theory for fact? A mild version of such a change has certainly come over me. To be parochial for a moment: no one will ever know what would have happened if by some fluke I had ended up in Oxford's nomothetic college, Nuffield, rather than in the idiographic St Antony's. However, I feel at home here, not just for reasons of style but for reasons of intellectual substance as well. The peculiar strength of St Antony's lies in the way in which its members bring historical depth and theoretical insights to bear on contemporary events. I like theory. Indeed I am not immune to the extravagant luxuries of non-Euclidean worlds of the human imagination. But as I grow older – and it has to be said that theory thrives on youth, so that ageing may be the real change which I am describing – I feel more and more strongly about what I like to call social analysis. Bringing processes and constellations not just to life, but to meaning, making sense of them, is a supreme challenge which requires the empathy of the historian as well as the tidy mind of the theorist. History has no meaning, said Karl Popper, but we can give it meaning, and we can do so in two ways: by social analysis, and by moral action.

On second thoughts, the Toynbee Prize seemed no longer so puzzling. My truly distinguished predecessors as prizewinners were all seeking the wholesome art of social analysis and moral action. Perhaps I may be allowed to single out Raymond Aron, who was my mentor and friend. More than ever do I admire his ability to steer a course of reason – of good-humoured reason at that – through the temptations of a century which would have tested even St Antony of Egypt. It took courage, courage of mind and of heart, to walk the lonely path of liberty and sheer good sense when all your friends fell under the spell of one or the other of the ideologies of the time. We are fortunate in Oxford in having among us one of the few for whom this has remained true throughout, Isaiah Berlin. The names of such great men, more than anything that I am going to say, stand for the intention of these remarks which I have called, 'citizens in search of meaning'.

One other comment on the Prize, or rather on the man in whose name it is given, is in place. The Prize itself mentions contributions to social science. Arnold Toynbee was not exactly a pure historian. For one thing he held a chair at the place which will forever command my special affection, the London School of Economics. For another thing, Toynbee was not only what some in this college call, 'Chatham Housey', indeed the Director of Studies at the Royal Institute of International Affairs and thus close to the fashions of today, but his dominant concern was to discover pattern and significance in widely disparate events. When I leafed through my copy of the abridged *Study of History* (given to me by Captain Brian Luxton, an officer in the British Forces, as part of the 're-education' of a young German after the war), I found tucked away in the back the notes which I made while listening to a lecture by Arnold Toynbee in Hamburg on 1 November 1949. His subject at the time had to do with social laws and personal liberty. Professional historians are sceptical when it comes to laws of decline or of progress (so Toynbee argued), but there are recurrences and continuities which result from the laws which govern human affairs. Uniformity arises, rises perhaps, from our unconscious depths. And liberty? There are subjects, and there are lawmakers. The lecturer seemed in rather a hurry to move from ordinary citizens to the divine lawgiver. 'If man can make his will conform to that of God he is master rather than slave of the laws governing human life', I noted from Toynbee's 1949 lecture, not without question marks of faint disapproval even by the 20-year-old.

My remarks today are inspired by events which are relevant to such observations. There are times when history itself seems to become social science. This is a cryptic statement. What I mean is that certain events raise issues of such fundamental significance that they defy the normal skills of story-telling. Wars and revolutions suspend all normal assumptions. Wars take us to the raw bones of human relations in more senses than one, and I for one believe that there is little to be gained by seeing them exposed. Revolutions raise fundamental issues of the social contract. What is the cement that holds human societies together? How do we go about building constitutions, and constitutions of liberty at that? Today I am not going to speak about the war in which we may find ourselves entangled in the Middle East before the anniversary of the breach of the Berlin Wall, or at any rate that of Vaclav Havel's surprising translation from the Magic Lantern theatre to the Hradshin. But I am going to speak about an aspect of the experience of the revolution of 1989. As you may know, I have written about it with passion and enthusiasm. It was a wonderful time to be alive. Today, however, my concern is with a worrying aspect of the process, and one which challenges historians and social scientists alike.

Let me start my argument by confessing to an embarrassment which I have suffered during this year of change. One of the subjects which have been raised in East Central Europe, in the Soviet Union and elsewhere is that of the self-determination of peoples. The notion goes back to the nineteenth century, but at least since President Wilson's Fourteen Points it has played a major, and often disturbing, role in international affairs. The principle is simple, at least at first sight. It says that people should have the right to determine their own affairs rather than have them determined by others: a Habsburg Emperor, a colonial Governor representing a distant Sovereign, a General Secretary of the Communist Party of the Soviet Union. This sounds, and in some ways is, alright. There are, however, ambiguities. People or peoples? The sudden transition, during the Monday demonstrations in Leipzig last November, from *Wir sind das Volk*, 'We are the people', to *Wir sind ein Volk*, 'We are one people', is not just one from democracy to nationalism. It also uses 'people' in two very different ways, as a society of citizens first, and as a somewhat mystical community second, *demos* and *thymos* perhaps, *Gesellschaft* and *Gemeinschaft* certainly. People in the first sense clearly have rights, civil rights, citizenship rights. But what about people in the second sense? Is their self-determination a notion, a political objective, is it a principle, or is it a right?

The practical problem with all so-called collective rights is that someone has to claim them on behalf of others. Once anything is claimed on behalf of others the probability must be high that some of the others do not feel represented by the leader or the agency making the claim. There are, fortunately for liberty if not always for those concerned, dissidents, minorities. What happens to them if a formerly dependent people claims self-determination? What happens to Russians in Estonia? 'Sociological research shows [I heard an Estonian MP say at a conference on nationalities] that it takes two generations for minorities to be absorbed into the majority culture.' So far, so good; but she added: 'Obviously we cannot give minorities in Estonia full rights until this process is completed.' Estonia is a relatively harmless case. Just think of Latvia, or of the Ukraine, to say nothing of the regions of Central Asia. Now that we see the Soviet Union, and even before it Yugoslavia, dissolve under our eyes, where does self-determination begin and end? The Moldavians want to be a part of Romania? In that case the Gagausians want to have an independent republic. There are more than twenty autonomous regions within the Russian Republic alone, and some include regions within regions. Do they all have the right to self-determination?

No doubt some will become independent states, the Baltic States among them. However, while the growing number of potential members of the United Nations, of countries, may be a nuisance and lead to extensive refurbishments on the East River, it is not the central problem. There is more cause for concern as one thinks back to the history of some of these new and not-so-new countries. People have conveniently forgotten the internal dimension of interwar independence, for example in the Baltics. What reason is there to believe that these countries have shed their anti-democratic past and will not return to variants of fascism? Not all leaders of the independence movements of 1990 inspire confidence.

This takes us to an even deeper problem. Many of those who invoke self-determination are seeking political communities which are homogeneous. Lithuanians have to be Catholics, though Estonians must not be that. Moldavians have to be Romanians. The Hungarian prime minister says that he is the prime minister of 14 million Hungarians; since Hungary proper has only 11 million inhabitants, this must mean that his colleagues in Bucharest and Prague (or perhaps Bratislava) are not the prime ministers of ethnic Hungarians in their midst. Cultural homogeneity is often the hard core of the demand for self-determination. Now there is nothing wrong with cultural homogeneity – or is there? Is it perhaps Japan's greatest problem on the road to liberal democracy that the assumption of homogeneity (stated with brutal explicitness by former prime minister Nakasone when he said that Japan had no human rights problems because it was a homogeneous country) is built into the foundations of the state, with immediate results for Japanese Koreans and indirect consequences for all? Does perhaps one of the weaknesses of the often-quoted example of Scandinavian countries lie in the assumption of homogeneity which has made it very difficult for Swedes to deal with relatively small immigrant communities? 'From entirely equals no state can emerge', said Aristotle. Could it be that from cultural equals no liberal state can emerge?

This is a large and difficult issue. I do not propose to advance facile precepts of heterogeneity. The advantages of living in a multicultural society are easier to enjoy for those who can withdraw to their country cottage, or even their own town house, than for those living in terraces or high-rise flats. The fact that most people do not like the multicultural world is not to be discounted. People like to be among their own. They are at ease there. It makes them feel at home. And of course people should feel at home when they are at home. Yet the world is not made of cosy homes in which all feel at ease among their own. The stranger is one of the earliest and most important figures of human history. His odyssey may be the source of suffering and tragedy, but it also forces people to think about themselves rather than just be themselves. This is not said wistfully, on the contrary. It may well be that people prefer the easy company of their peers; but then it may be that they prefer entropy. The tribe is both the past which we have fortunately left and our eternal dream. Immanuel Kant made the point with words which cannot be quoted too often when he spoke, in his 'Idea for a Universal History With Cosmopolitan Intent', of man's 'unsociable sociability'. People like the harmony of community. Yet if they had it, they would 'live an Arcadian, pastoral existence of perfect concord, self-sufficiency and mutual love. But all human talents would remain hidden forever in a dormant state, and people, as good-natured as the sheep they tended, would scarcely render their existence more valuable than that of their animal flocks.' Heterogeneity means antagonism and conflict; it means that ways and means have to be found to regulate conflict, constitutions; but by the same token it means that men and women come into their own as such, as humans. Variety, heterogeneity, difference are the stuff from which human progress is made.

The occasion may justify a personal comment. I have quoted Kant's thesis in several of my writings from 'Out of Utopia' to *The Modern Social Conflict*. Along with the last chapter of Karl Popper's *Open Society* it epitomizes my own approach to social and political analysis. The theory of conflict which I espoused as a young sociologist belongs squarely in this context. Conflict is the great stimulus of change, and our task in a world in which change is our only hope is to domesticate conflict by rules, by the constitution of liberty. Popper was right to pay so much attention to the enemies of the open society. They are of two kinds. There are those moderns who seek to impose their dogma. Claims for total power, monopoly power have to be fought with every fibre of our existence if we want to be human and free. But there is also the eternal dream of the tribe (in Karl Popper's terms), or of Arcadia (in Immanuel Kant's). Total power will fail in the end, though the cost may be almost unbearable; in a sense the whole century which is now passing away has been about this price, about Auschwitz and Gulag, about the uncounted dead of the wars. The eternal dream remains an eternal challenge. It challenges our ability to live with conflict, and more, to live decently with conflict.

This is not just a moral precept, but can be put in terms of social analysis. Perhaps there is no greater progress in terms of Kant and Popper than the realization of the idea of citizenship. I am using the term as my teacher T.H. Marshall used it in his Cambridge Lectures of 1950 on *Citizenship and Social Class*. Citizenship defines the floor on which all members of human society stand. Ideally, this means all humans, just like that. Immanuel Kant's 'world civil society' is in the end the only valid answer to the basic equality of the rank and the rights of all human beings. Short of a world civil society, we are creating substitutes, civil societies within boundaries, thus imperfect civil societies which involve definitions, exclusions, privileges and deprivations. Still, they are the best we have got so far, nation-states in which civil rights are guaranteed. If we are lucky, or rather if we are successful in our endeavours, we may be able to establish multinational civil rights in some parts of the world, as in Europe, though we have not yet done so. The European Community in particular (contrary to its antecedents, and notably the Council of Europe) is about protecting vested interests rather than creating citizenship rights. In all cases, citizenship is about giving people who differ in age and sex, in their beliefs and the colour of their skins, in their social interests and political preferences, the same basic entitlements. Such entitlements include what have come to be called, human rights, such as the integrity of the person and free speech; they also include the civil rights of participation in the political community, the labour market, society; and they include the right to pursue one's own cultural preferences. Citizenship defines in practical, almost legal terms what all human beings have in common, in order to set people free to be different. The floor on which people stand in a society of citizens is common to all of them but the building in which they live has many storeys and apartments and nooks and crannies within them.

This is, I believe, an exhilarating idea which defines an entire agenda for freedom. But then I have just confessed to what many would regard as a rather austere morality of living with conflict. The fact is that somehow citizenship does not seem to catch the hearts of people. Some have tried to turn the concept into one with greater appeal to our feelings. A Speaker's Commission in Britain has explored what is fashionably called, 'active citizenship', that is the citizen as a contributor to the commonwealth rather than just a recipient of its fruits. Clearly, appeals to duties and obligations touch the heart more than the insistence on rights. 'Do not ask what America can do for you, ask what you can do for America ...' Attractive as this twist may sound, it is also misleading. The whole point about citizenship is that it provides an instrument for living with difference. Undoubtedly, citizens have obligations as well as entitlements. However, for one thing they must not be seen as conditions for each other, or else we end up with perversions like 'no representation without taxation'. For another thing, if citizenship is used to mobilize all for a common purpose, it is turned against its original intent.

In the new democracies of East Central Europe this is well understood. The advocates of civil society are not usually the protagonists of a return to the tribe. Yet there are many who have this dream. While the honeymoon of the revolution of '89 was also a time in which the notion of a 'civic forum' could thrive, the place of the protagonists of citizenship is now taken by other forces. The founder of the great civic movement Solidarnosc in Poland turns into a politician who invokes anti-intellectual resentments, if not worse. The author of the greatest indictment of Stalinism turns into an advocate of primeval and tribal Russian values. So-called liberals in Slovenia explicitly advocate the emancipation of the 'national person' rather than the real person, the individual. Electoral turnout suggests that the rules of the game of the open society have lost their initial appeal rather quickly. Moreover, the nation in the emphatic, tribal rather than the constitutional sense is at times coupled with another deep emotion which is that of religion. The appeal of those who do not like the dissociation of Caesar from God, or vice versa, is by no means confined to the Islamic world. Citizens, it appears, or would-be citizens, have become afraid of their chances and instead embrace archaic ideas.

These are sentiments which cannot be dismissed lightly. As the heavy hand of *nomenklatura* socialism lifts, people remember where they belong, or at least where they once belonged. In any case, the open lands of freedom are not enough. They are an uncharted territory, and in order to give it contours, and thereby make sense of the direction in which one is moving, co-ordinates are needed, lines of demarcation and of orientation. Citizenship, the open society, the constitution of liberty do not provide these by themselves. They are all opportunities for choice, chances, marvellous chances to be sure, but mere chances too. Individuals need an inner compass to guide them, and for the compass to work there have to be magnetic fields outside which enable us to distinguish between north and south, right and wrong, desirable and undesirable courses of action, and even the shades of grey in between.

Chances are incomplete as long as they are merely options. Only if certain deep structures – I have called them, ligatures – are added, do they become chances with meaning, life chances. The world of ligatures is a minefield for liberals. Most deep structures have an absolute quality: they do not readily recognize shades of grey. People either belong or they do not, and if they do not, they have no claim to rights. The nation in its emphatic sense – by contrast to the nation-state as the repository of the rule of law – has given rise to boundary disputes, internal divisions and wars. Religion as a political force has been a great destructive force of history as well as a source of structures of meaning. And both are once again with us. A new wave of nationalism is not confined to East Central Europe, and religious fundamentalism is not confined to the world of Islam. As familiar structures dissolve, the search for meaning becomes more hectic, and people are only too ready to fall for the lure of ancient definitions.

This is a wide and treacherous field, and not one, I confess, in which I find it easy to tread. Was it Max Weber who said that in matters of religion his musical ear tended to desert him? But perhaps it helps to return for a moment to the issue of self-determination. Why is citizenship, why is even the open society not enough for those who have escaped the fangs of imperial and ideological hegemony? Why do they seek the arcadia of the tribe, of homogeneous nations? Because without deep structures of belonging, the new options appear to have little meaning. This is where the critical question arises: is the open society of citizens then an impossible project? Is it bound to run up against the need for ligatures which almost by definition introduce elements of closure, boundaries, definitions? Or can open societies have a meaningful identity?

When Jeane Kirkpatrick wrote her article in 1979 on the subject of 'Dictatorships and Double Standards', she put forward a curious argument. Democracy, she said, far from being a universal trend or even need, was really a form of social and political organization peculiar to the Anglo-Saxon world: to Britain, the United States and the temperate Commonwealth countries. It was pointless to try and persuade others to follow the same route, a sociological fallacy (which she imputed above all to President Carter's adviser Zbigniew Brzezinski and his theories of modernization). The only relevant question about the rest of the world was: are they for us or are they against us? The argument was sufficiently outrageous to earn her a post in President Reagan's first government. But outrageous though it is, it is neither totally absurd nor is Mrs Kirkpatrick the only one who subscribes to it.

Why did – and perhaps still does – democracy, the open society, the society of citizens work in Britain and the United States? What are the deep structures which appear to give meaning to people's choices? In the United States one is reminded of that civic religion, or perhaps the role of religion in civil society, which Tocqueville has pointed out to such effect. The social conformism of religious nonconformism is, or was, one of the bonds which held the country together. In the older small towns of New England, half a dozen or more churches would be lined up in the same street, with different denominations but the same openness for visitors, the same sense of community responsibility and probably much the same liturgy. When public speakers say, 'God Bless America' – and they do so often – their audience may think of many gods, but they are linked in one America. The flag and the constitution enter into a holy alliance with a remarkably secular religion which without being ecumenical manages to unite rather than divide.

The British experience is more complicated. Edmund Burke's 'primeval contract of eternal society' made me think about it, as did the disdain with which he considered the revolution in France as if to say: who do they think they are, believing that they can create a democratic society? This Kirkpatrick strand of thinking is still very much alive, as the undertones of the debate

about Britain and Europe show. On this island things are different ... the
implication is not nationalist; for a long time, there was a considerable
generosity towards those who came to throw in their lot with the locals; but
it is an unspoken assumption that 'we are the chosen people'. Indeed,
continuity is the essence of the ligatures which underly citizenship and the
open society in Britain. A constitutional principle like 'the sovereignty of
the Queen in Parliament' expresses this well: the Sovereign is still there, but
he or she has chosen to allow her prerogative to be exercised by an elected
parliament. Britain's most brilliant contribution to social and political history
may well be the combination of old institutions with new needs.

Yet as such statements are made, the temptation, alas! the need is always
there to slip from the present to the past tense. At the very least, these things
are changing. In Britain, what is arguably the most anti-traditional government
in its history has gone out of its way to crush traditions which had already
begun to crumble. In the United States, we increasingly find heterogeneity
without community. Americans have all become hyphenated; now they have
to be Italian-Americans, Chinese-Americans, African-Americans. As a
result, Britain and America are increasingly faced with the self-same issue
which bewitches the new democracies and others in the world: how can we
have an open society of citizens which captures the hearts as well as the minds
of people without destroying by emotion what it has created by reason? What
ligatures give the options of liberty meaning?

One country in which this subject has been fiercely debated and is of
immediate significance, is Germany. (Germany should actually be credited
with the intelligence and intensity of its public debates of its history and
identity even if outsiders are sometimes puzzled by the *Historikerstreit* and
its more recent sequel.) Some have fallen for a totally implausible tribalism
of the two states of yesteryear, the FRG and the GDR. Günter Grass has
managed to combine this nostalgia with a vague though highly emotional
Europeanism which others, notably outside Germany, rightly find suspicious.
European dreams are no substitute for real ligatures. Jürgen Habermas has
taken up an originally conservative concept in this context, 'constitutional
patriotism'. He of course has in mind a kind of Rousseauean *volonté générale*
which is established by permanent discourse and sustains the basic laws. This
may be asking too much, though among the young, Habermas's contribution
can hardly be overrated. One could return the concept, however, to its
original meaning which has to do with pride in the spirit of the laws and the
institutions created in its name. One cannot and should not love governments,
but I suppose it is possible to feel great affection for a particular way of
separating powers, and of enabling and controlling them at the same time.

And yet, constitutional patriotism remains a *Kopfgeburt*, a thing of the mind, not of the heart. It does not satisfy the need of many to live by and pass on to future generations deep structures of life in society. You will not have failed to notice that I am reaching the end of my reflections without having offered an answer to one of the major questions of our time. For two centuries it seemed good enough to devote the energies of liberty to the creation of wider options for more people, and to relegate deeper structures to the private sphere, or simply to assume their existence. Perhaps this is still good enough. If it is not, we are in trouble. Whatever citizenship and the open society are, they are not a new religion. In this respect too, Burke was right and the French Revolution was wrong. It remains important to know what we do not want, which is any kind of closure, of monopoly and of dogma. We have to hold on to the values of citizenship in open societies. But it is hard to deny that the question of meaning remains unanswered in East and West, and the search for an answer may well provide the subject of the struggles of the next phase of history.

The Good Society

4   The Good Society

First 1949 Seminar Memorial Lecture, delivered at the London School of Economics and Political Science on 19 November 1992

Utopia expired in the final weeks of the memorable year, 1989. She had been poorly for some time, and few attempts were made to save her life. On the contrary, a sense of good riddance spread from libraries stocked with 'The Open Society and Its Enemies' and 'The God that Failed' to the Round Tables and then the streets of Warsaw and Budapest, Leipzig and Prague. Thus she went out, surprisingly perhaps, with a bang and not with a whimper. She? One might well think of Utopia as the tenth muse, the muse of dreams, albeit of dreams which have a tendency to turn into nightmares. 'The real question is,' Joachim Fest wrote about recent events, 'whether all dreams of a New Order, be they oriented to the past or to a "goal of history" inevitably end in terror whatever their original motive may have been'. And he gave the answer too: 'What is left of the Utopian efforts is little more than an unending trail of horror which has imprinted itself on our minds as a traumatic experience.' The 'harvest of sorrow', Gulag, Auschwitz. Total visions of social order produce totalitarian realities. Who is to say whether this could happen again? But for the moment, Utopia is gone, and another muse, Clio, far from having suffered her own demise, is back in full force. Some begin to feel that if anything we are seeing too much history after the collapse of the old assumptions.

The noise and the drama of these events has almost drowned out another departure though one that occurred with a whimper: the passing away of 'democratic planning' designed to turn the 'great society' into one that is also good in some sense. At the London School of Economics these are familiar notions. The School was never the home of Utopian dreams; it was therefore never threatened by the two great totalitarian nightmares of the century. But LSE was the home of another characteristic and now defunct approach to social affairs, from the Webbs to Beveridge and on to Karl Mannheim and Richard Titmuss and others. One might vary the famous Fabian motto – 'Educate! Organize! Agitate!' – for this approach: Investigate! Educate! Planify! There are social problems. The first task is to study them thoroughly. The facts brought up by such investigations speak for themselves. They must, of course, be disseminated. The general public needs to be prepared for change, and even more importantly, experts need to be trained as agents of change. Such change is the responsibility of governments. The solution of social problems requires a concerted effort of men and women of knowledge and good will to create a machinery of improvement, including income transfers, public services, offices of planning and systems of implementation.

This was a noble hope, and one that has led to important and lasting changes. However, insofar as this hope implied a comprehensive view of human purpose and social organization, it has come to grief in the 1970s and 1980s if not earlier. Few now believe that humans are able, or should even try to organize their affairs comprehensively and by deliberate action. There is what has been called, the 'cost of good intentions', both financial and social. There is the new dependency of a welfare state which endeavours to guide people from the cradle to the grave. There is the effect of the leaden hand of bureaucracy on human creativity. And then there are the deeper objections which were first voiced by H.G. Wells in his beautiful satire *The New Machiavelli* of 1911: '"Order, education, discipline," said Sir Graham. "Excellent things! But I've a sort of memory – in my young days we talked about something called liberty!"'

Wells meant the Webbs of course, whom he called the Baileys: 'With a sort of frantic energy they were trying to develop that sham expert officialdom of theirs to plan, regulate and direct the affairs of humanity ... They were neglecting human life altogether in social organization.' Forty-five years later, in 1956, Anthony Crosland took up the theme of the threats to 'liberty and gaiety in private life':

> We need not only higher exports and old-age pensions, but more open-air cafés, brighter and gayer streets at night, later closing-hours for public houses, more local repertory theatres ... The enemy in all this will often be in unexpected guise; it is not only dark Satanic things and people that now bar the road to the new Jerusalem, but also, if not mainly, hygienic, respectable, virtuous things and people, lacking only in grace and gaiety.

Thus, these arguments are not new. They are indeed the main theme of the splendid book which gave this lecture its title, Walter Lippman's *The Good Society* which was first published in 1938, and then again in 1943. Lippman's central argument is that liberalism was on the right path in the nineteenth century, but then stopped in its tracks and became a barren defence of the status quo. Collectivism filled the resulting vacuum of ideas. But collectivism erred in both its absolute and its gradual version. The former led to fascism and communism; Lippman's indictment of the totalitarian potential of Utopian dreams is every bit as forceful as Popper's a few years later. However, the latter, 'gradual collectivism' through planning has its own 'tragic irony': 'Because a planned society must be one in which the people obey their rulers, there can be no plan to find the planners.' They might be 'benevolent despots'. 'On the other hand they might not be.' Liberty is the victim.

What then is the good society? Lippman makes a powerful case, and he makes it in passionate language. I have no disagreement with this argument and much admiration for its counter-cyclical thrust at a time of totalitarian temptations. Yet neither the power nor the passion can detract from the gaps which remain. Walter Lippman's central point is that liberalism has to be freed from the errors of *laissez-faire* thinking. Liberalism is about rules, about the rule of law in the best and fullest sense. This has to be invoked to protect people not only from arbitrary dominion but also from vested interests, from cartels, and from distortions of the market by private power. In a key section of the chapter on 'The Agenda of Liberalism' Lippman surveys 'The Field of Reform'. Here he speaks of the importance of small businesses, the need for the conservation of land, of social insurance and other such matters. The thrust of all this is to turn the Great Society in Graham Wallas's sense, that is the interdependent world society based on the modern division of labour, into a – and perhaps, *the* – Good Society.

Lippman uses capital letters for this project, but he is reluctant to tell us much about it. 'The Good Society has no architectural design. There are no blueprints. There is no mould in which human life is to be shaped. Indeed, to expect the blueprint of such a mould is a mode of thinking against which the liberal temper is in constant protest.' This sounds fine, notably for the student of Popper which I am proud to be. Thus I certainly agree that 'the supreme architect, who begins as a visionary, becomes a fanatic and ends as a despot', is a dangerous creature. But can we really stop here? Is this all we want to say about the good society? I shall demonstrate, at least in passing, that Lippman himself did not, in fact, stop at this point; but let me first take the simpler route of quoting two authors who are less reluctant to describe their good society without fancying themselves as 'supreme architects' let alone despots.

The first is Graham Wallas, the man who declined to become the founding Director of LSE and thereby almost quelled the idea, but who went on to teach at the School and who wrote in 1914, *The Great Society*. Wallas praises Aristotle: 'virtue is rightly defined as a Mean, and yet in so far as it aims at the highest excellence, it is an Extreme'. He then develops this idea:

> If I try to make for myself a visual picture of the social system which I should desire for England and America, there comes before me a recollection of those Norwegian towns and villages where everyone, the shopkeepers and the artisans, the schoolmaster, the boy who drove the post-

ponies, and the student daughter of the innkeeper who took round the potatoes, seemed to respect themselves, to be capable of Happiness as well as of pleasure and excitement, because they were near the Mean in the employment of all their faculties. I can imagine such people learning to exploit the electric power from their waterfalls, and the minerals in their mountains, without dividing themselves into dehumanized employers or officials, and equally dehumanized 'hands'. But I recollect also that the very salt and savour of Norwegian life depends on the fact that poets, and artists, and statesmen have worked in Norway with a devotion which was not directed by any formula of moderation.

Three-quarters of a century later, another somewhat reluctant leader of liberal persuasion, Václav Havel, let his fertile imagination roam as he thought about 'the kind of Czechoslovakia I would like to see and strive for with my limited power'. The entire chapter of Havel's *Summer Meditations* would be worth quoting, but even a short excerpt gives the flavour of Havel's good society:

> Life in the towns and villages will have overcome the legacy of greyness, uniformity, anonymity, and ugliness inherited from the totalitarian era. It will have a genuinely human dimension. Every main street will have at least two bakeries, two sweet-shops, two pubs, and many other small shops, all privately owned and independent. Thus the streets and neighbourhoods will regain their unique face and atmosphere. Small communities will naturally begin to form again, communities centred on the street, the apartment block, or the neighbourhood. People will once more begin to experience the phenomenon of home ... Prefabricated high-rise apartment blocks and other kinds of gigantic public housing developments will no longer be built ... In short, the villages and towns will once again begin to have their own distinctive appearance, culture, style, cleanliness, and beauty. We can't expect to become a Switzerland or a Holland; we will remain ourselves, but our outer face will stand comparison with these countries.

Different though they are, these visions have important features in common. One is the idyllic streak which will need further exploration. Another is the comparison with other countries of a particular size and kind – Norway, Switzerland, Holland. More recently, and before the collapse of its model, Sweden figured for many as the epitome of the good society, but never the United States, or even Britain or France, although these are the countries which have attracted immigrants over a long time. Both Graham Wallas and Václav Havel have made their peace with modernity, but it turns out to be a shallow peace because nostalgia for 'the boy who drove the post-ponies' and main streets with 'two bakeries, two sweet-shops, two pubs' is never far away. Walter Lippman may have been wise to be cautious and not tell us of his dreams, but as I pursue three lines of analysis of these images of the good society by critical minds, his own vision begins to look ever more similar.

Let me remind you: we have left Utopia and the totalitarian nightmare which it promoted behind, and also the great deception of benevolent gradual collectivism. We are now looking at the way in which the good society is seen without the risk of totalitarian rule or even the need for comprehensive planning. Still, the visions quoted suggest a world which is curiously static. One cannot really imagine why Havel's Czechoslovakia should ever change once it is achieved ('in ten, fifteen or twenty years,' as he said in 1991, though it took only another year for the real Czechoslovakia to fall apart). And while Wallas's Norwegians were to exploit 'electric power from their waterfalls' (he could hardly foresee the oil at the bottom of the North Sea), there will be no significant stratification, let alone class conflict as a result. The good society is seen as a steady state rather than a process, a defined and definitive condition which can be achieved rather than a continuation of the muddle and the untidiness of affairs here and now.

Walter Lippman has a telling passage in his 'Agenda of Liberalism' in which he speaks of mobility. He clearly favours mobility of capital. While he accepts that not everybody can stay in the same place forever, 'the tides of population must move slowly if old communities are not to be devitalized by emigration and new communities overwhelmed by unassimilable immigration. It should, therefore, be the aim of public policy to mitigate this human evil by using social controls to induce inanimate capital, rather than living men to achieve high mobility.' This is certainly not the American way of life, indeed it sounds like a positively anti-American defence of homogeneity. The subject is topical enough, and it is important to refrain from scoring cheap points. There are degrees of migration which are necessary and even desirable, but a point may well come when communities either lose their identity or are no longer able to assimilate newcomers. But mobility surely is one of the key elements of liberty and life chances, and a static society soon becomes stagnant in social as well as in economic terms.

Curiously, entropy is not just a deadly risk but also an object of human desire. Even economists have, when they allowed themselves to dream, generally come up with versions of the 'stationary state'. From John Stuart Mill to the limits-to-growth theorists of the 1970s, the idea has charmed them. Even John Maynard Keynes, in his famous *aperçu* about 'Economic Possibilities for Our Grandchildren', mused about a time when the economic problem is resolved. People do not need to work much any more; they are all quite well off; the love of money is 'recognized for what it is, a somewhat disgusting morbidity'. So what will people do? For a fleeting moment Keynes entertains the idea that there may be a great collective 'nervous breakdown'; but then another vision gets the better of his realism: 'We shall once more value ends above means and prefer the good to the useful. We shall honour those who can teach us how to pluck the hour and the day virtuously and well, the delightful people who are capable of taking direct enjoyment in things, the lilies of the field who toil not, neither do they spin.'

A lovely world – or is it? I cannot help thinking of the useful irony with which Immanuel Kant, over two hundred years ago, mocked the human desire to 'live an Arcadian, pastoral existence of perfect concord, self-sufficiency and mutual love'. This would mean, Kant argues in his 'Idea for a Universal History With Cosmopolitan Intent', that 'all human talents would remain hidden forever in a dormant state, and people, as good-natured as the sheep they tended, would scarcely render their existence more valuable than that of their animal flocks'. Kant goes on to praise man's 'unsociable sociability' as the stimulus for progress. 'Thanks be to Nature then for the incompatibility, for the heartless competitive vanity, for the insatiable desire to possess and to rule.'

We are imperfect, and we are living in a world of uncertainty. Advancing our life chances is therefore a matter of trial and error, of conflict and change. The open society with its untidiness, its antagonisms, its discomforts, and above all its constitutional openness, its forever unfinished character, is the good society. Arcadia in the end is no less a threat than Utopia and the well-planned state.

Keynes introduced into his vision another element which leads to a second reflection. He wants us 'to return to some of the most sure and certain principles of religion and traditional virtue'. Us? What does he mean? Does he mean individuals, or is he drawing the map of a society guided by these principles in its institutions as it were? Walter Lippman too sings the praises of human virtue. 'There must be a strong desire to be just.' 'There must be moral standards which discourage the quest for privilege and the exercise of arbitrary power.' 'There must be patience and tolerance and kindness in hearing claims, in argument, in negotiation, and in reconciliation.' Such virtues, he argues, have always been practised, though not by enough people and not to a sufficient extent. Still, they have been shown by 'enough men in great enough degree to have given mankind here and there and for varying periods of time the intimations of a Good Society'.

Individual human beings clearly can be good, and they can be evil. Moral philosophers may differ on what exactly this means, but in everyday life we have a fairly shrewd idea of what is good and what is evil. The man who killed the woman commuter did an evil deed, and the person who looks after dying aids patients is doing good deeds. Nor is it difficult to agree with Keynes and with Lippman that it is good to remain untainted by greed and the lust for power, though here one begins to wonder about Max Weber's distinction between the saint and the politician, the 'ethics of conviction' and the 'ethics of responsibility'. Does it make sense to use moral categories for institutions, or even for collectivities? We readily speak of good and bad governments, but most of the time these are judgements of competence and of preference rather than morals. Sometimes governments are run by morally offensive people; President Collor of Brazil is a recent example of that condition. Sometimes governments seem to encourage immoral behaviour; the deepest doubts in the Reagan–Thatcher era have to do with this suspicion. But in all these cases moral judgements refer to individuals, not institutions. The distinction becomes more difficult as we consider governments which are responsible for horrendously evil acts like Hitler's regime. It is no accident that the notion of the 'collective guilt of Germans' emerged when the extent of Nazi crimes became evident. Yet I wonder whether this makes sense. Collective responsibility, certainly, collective shame, yes, but if guilt and repentance are turned into collective categories, they not only relieve individuals somehow of their share of evil but also become metaphors rather than effective judgements.

This must not be misunderstood. I cannot stand governments which tolerate or encourage immoral actions, corrupt governments whose members are lying. I believe that governments can set a moral tone and therefore like it if President Clinton introduces a particularly strict code of ethics for his appointees. Indeed, there is a risk that Max Weber's distinction is taken as an excuse for morally unacceptable actions. The word, *Realpolitik*, is rightly viewed with suspicion.

Yet there is a problem if the attempt is made to turn morality into public policy. This is partly the problem of 'The New Machiavelli' but there is more to it. I shall call it the Singapore Syndrome because Singapore is perhaps the most extreme example of a society which endeavours to enforce private goodness by public sanctions. It all sounds quite harmless:

The Community Development Section was set up in July 1980 to assist Residents' Committees (RCs) in public housing estates to promote social cohesiveness and self-reliance within their communities. The Section conducts training courses to train RC members on the techniques of community development and the execution of neighbourhood projects. It also promotes and develops community-based projects such as the

Befriender Service whereby residents in the estates lend help to their aged neighbours who do not have relatives to care for them.

And so on, in an official Government Handbook for Singapore (1985) which also tells us that 81 per cent of the people live in Housing and Development Board (HDB) run homes, nicely sorted into racial groups according to national quotas. 'The public housing programme has continued its vigorous expansion through the greater use of prefabricated and industrialized methods of construction.' Not exactly Václav Havel's good society! But is it good at all to make people be good, or perhaps just appear to be good? Is it good to fine them heavily for littering the streets and force them to use public transport rather than private cars? Examples of the Singapore Syndrome can be found elsewhere. When Helmut Schmidt was German Federal Chancellor he toyed with the idea of introducing a television-free day. What about 'busing' children to other parts of town in order to promote racially mixed schools? Indeed, what about Citizens' Charters which do not stipulate rights but moral obligations?

Let us give the perpetrators of the Singapore Syndrome the benefit of the doubt and assume that their intention is to create a good society. Even so, the translation of morality into public policy leads to a curiously stifling condition. Singapore itself is an example. Opposition parties have tried in vain to gain a foothold in parliament, and the banning of the *Far Eastern Economic Review* is only the most visible part of a censorship which tends to accompany governments which try, or perhaps pretend, to be moral. Soon after the red-light district had been pulled down, the government of Singapore hired 'love boats' to send young couples out to sea for purposes which, in the 1920s and 1930s, would have been called Eugenics. Citizens' Charters are harmless instruments by comparison; but there is a tendency both in the United States and in Britain to emphasize not the rights but the obligations of citizens which is never far from telling people what to do even if it travels under the title, *Encouraging Citizenship*. It is good for people to work (so one argument goes), they should therefore not be entitled to transfer incomes unless they work (so it continues), in the end they will have to be made to work.

I find it easy to agree with Walter Lippman in his critique of a vested-interest notion of *laissez faire* which simply does not care for those in need. But when it comes to morality, I should prefer to leave it to preachers and philosophers rather than governments, to friends and neighbours rather than a state-organized Befriender Service; it should ultimately be left to individuals. The institutions of the open society are convenient in view of human frailty; they allow the correction of errors without bloodshed; they are thus a pretty good invention of civilized humans. However, they work best if we do not try to instil any morality – or indeed ideology – in them. I for one prefer London, warts and all, to the censorious hygiene of Singapore.

Yet there is still one – the third – line of analysis which needs to be pursued to make sense of that elusive concept, the good society. Do I really prefer London as it is today? What about the streets strewn with rubbish, the potholes, the dirt and the noise? What about the homeless in the doorways of the Strand? What about the absence of civic sense among the citizens of London? (Actually, what do notions like 'civic sense' and 'civic virtues' mean in our context?) In what sense are there citizens of London? Who can they have recourse to, which government can they sack when they are unhappy with the prevailing state of affairs? Let me return, for a serious if not a simple answer, to the quotations with which this analysis began. It is a striking fact that those who speak about the good society tend to think of local communities, and fairly small communities at that. Both Lippman and Havel refer to 'life in towns and villages', but Lippman's Norwegian town is not Oslo, and Havel's Czechoslovak town is not Prague. Some venture a little further. David Donnison has taken his heart into his hands and described what he regards as *The Good City*:

> To sum up, a city which provides both good opportunities for the less skilled and more vulnerable, and a distribution of opportunities between socio-economic groups which is not too unequal may typically be a *fairly* large town with varied, prosperous and expanding enterprises demanding some training and a wide range of middle grade skills, operating in an equilibrium with a housing market, an education system and other sectors of the urban economy and without major discontinuities within sectors or disjunctions between sectors. There would be good opportunities for the least skilled to improve their status and living conditions through training and in other ways, and a plentiful supply of the most skilled workers (managers, doctors, senior officials and so on) in relation to the demands for them. Monopoly and discrimination would be difficult to impose both in the political and the economic market places, and a large and thriving public sector would help to redistribute resources and to protect the most vulnerable people. The inflow of migrants with varied origins and traditions would be sufficient to create a plural society whose members learn to accept newcomers, and whose political leaders have an interest in gaining the support of minorities. This is an optimistic scenario, suggesting that the most equal city and the city which treats poor people best could be that same place.

The scenario is not only optimistic; it is also yet another example of the suspiciously idyllic nature of the good society, or rather, the good city, if in a social-science language which sounds somewhat less enticing than that of Václav Havel. Even so, Donnison's good city has two characteristics which are worth emphasizing. One is that it may be a little larger than Lippman's or Havel's, but it is still only a 'fairly large town' which is another way of saying that there is a degree of *Gemeinschaft*, of intensive community awareness in it. It is not London, nor is it a society in the larger sense. The other point is that people in the 'fairly large town' are nice both in themselves and to each other. Like Lippman's Norwegians they are 'near the Mean in the employment of all their faculties'. More than that, they are bent on improving themselves without wanting to do others down; they even accept minorities and newcomers happily as fellow citizens.

Leaving doubts and irony on one side, there is a serious point to all this. It is that the good society has to offer more than the Great Society or even the Open Society. The Great Society is the modern world, division of labour, interdependence and all. The Open Society is the world of democracy and the market economy, the constitution of liberty. Neither of these provides what Havel likes to call a home for people. They are in a sense like the functional glass and concrete structures to which we have grown accustomed, but in which it is hard to find a familiar and cosy place. The authors quoted here have tried to get round the dilemma by inventing small villages and towns, or at the most fairly large ones, within the Great and the Open Society; but in fact such places are few and far between, and where they exist they are often neither Great nor Open but remnants of an older layer of history. Our authors are looking for something important, indeed necessary, but one must doubt whether they have found it in the good city.

Robert Bellah has seen this problem in the book which he and four others published in 1991 on *The Good Society*. Bellah cites Graham Wallas and then John Dewey who, in 1927, voiced the concern that 'the Great Society has invaded and partially disintegrated the small communities of former times without generating a Great Community'. Bellah looks again at Walter Lippman's book and finds it both helpful and wanting. Indeed, he is more sceptical than Lippman about the belief 'that all our problems can be solved by autonomous individuals, a market economy, and a procedural state' and holds against it that panacea of the post-communist new left, communitarianism: 'Communitarians believe that more substantive ethical identities and a more active participation in a democratic polity are necessary for the functioning of any decent society.' However, Bellah realizes that the word 'communitarian' can easily be misunderstood as setting face-to-face groups against the state, the economy and larger structures in general. He therefore looks for other concepts, though ones inspired by the same intention.

The concepts which he offers are perhaps not immediately plausible. One is, the 'politics of generativity' by which he means concern for generations past and future, with 'social inclusion and participation' as the key theme, geared towards anchoring 'our economic and political institutions firmly in the moral discourse of citizens concerned about the common good and the long run'. Next, Bellah takes up Lippman's praise of virtue but wants it based on faith. To this end he quotes the 1986 letter of American Catholic bishops with its proposal of 'a thick, organic connection in our moral understanding of economic, political and spiritual life, centred around the necessity of communal solidarity and realizing the dignity and sacredness of all persons'. For good measure, Bellah adds Niebuhr's notion of responsibility based on trust. As 'members of the universal community of all being', we may not have superior wisdom but 'we can be, as Václav Havel defines his role, ambassadors of trust in a fearful world. When enough of us have sufficient trust to act responsibly, there is a chance to achieve, at least in part, a good society.'

Bellah is by no means the only one to demand a change of values. He wants us to turn from Lockean individualism to a modern kind of Rousseauean communitarianism, solidarity by discourse as it were (to use the language of Habermas). Communitarianism is actually the new collectivism; it responds to the individualism of the Thatcher world as collectivism did to that of Victorian times; and both are versions of what Isaiah Berlin has castigated as 'positive liberty'. Can one be sure that Bellah's prescriptions are not a recipe for fundamentalism? The French call it *integrisme*, religious belief which does not differentiate between God and Caesar but claims all. To many, it has its attractions. This is notably the case in the face of the relativism which often accompanies the society in which anything goes. In introducing a volume of *Philosophical Essays on the Ideas of a Good Society*, Yeager Hudson and Creighton Peden make much of the hope 'that rationally consistent and humanly beneficial ethical principles might be found and agreed upon as a basis for a better social order'. However, they hurry to add that of course there cannot be consensus on such principles. 'The point is to talk with conviction and to listen with openmindedness about the issues.' I am frankly more impressed by Ernest Gellner's ironic diatribe – it was in fact a King's College sermon! – on *The Uniqueness of Truth*. Gellner is equally scathing about Relativists and Fundamentalists. He holds against them the creed of Enlightenment Puritans, EPs, who believe in truth and goodness but do not think that anyone can claim to possess it, so that we have to rely on procedures of trial and error.

The Fundamentalist and the Enlightenment Puritan share a sense of and respect for the uniqueness of truth; the EP and the Relativist, share a penchant for tolerance; and the Relativist and the Fundamentalist, share a reasonably well furnished, habitable world, as opposed to the arid emptiness of the world of the EP.

Yet Gellner has no doubt about his place in this *ménage à trois* (as he calls it):

> If this story has any clear moral, it is that the future lies not with some secular counter-revelation, but rather in that ambiguous, unstable, uneasy relationship between Faith, Indifference, and Seriousness which I have tried to describe.

So where does that leave the Good Society and its friends? If I have quoted more authors more extensively than is usual in a lecture, the reason was not to hide behind their words. It was rather to trace some markers in the recent history of the idea of a good society and to illustrate its pitfalls and its ramifications. Fundamentally, I remain an individualist. I have my pangs of doubt about the Great Society like everyone else, but I accept that it is the real modern world. I have no doubts about the Open Society and am prepared to take on all relativists who see it as a rarefied luxury of a minority in a few lucky countries. In one sense, democracy and the market economy are desirable precisely because they are cold projects which do not make any claims on the souls of men and women. But I appreciate, increasingly perhaps, that so far as human society is concerned, this is not enough. We need conflict, and we need change, but we are threatened by anomy. This threat cannot be averted by normal politics. People need ligatures as well as options to enjoy full life chances, and ligatures require the variety of autonomous associations which we call, civil society. These associations are in a metaphorical sense the 'towns and villages', including some fairly large ones, in which face-to-face contacts are not impossible and solidarity prevails. Indeed, local autonomy is an indispensable element of a working civil society, along with independent universities, a free press and the rest. And it needs citizens who are not frightened but ready to stand up and be counted when basic values are under threat. Such citizens have to have what Karl Popper in a somewhat surprising phrase calls, at the end of the first volume of his *Open Society*, 'both security and freedom'. Looking at the history of mankind, such security will in part be provided by peace and prosperity, but in part by what, and perhaps even whether, people believe, that is by bonds which through civil society reach into deep culture without ever denying the necessity and dignity of the constitution of liberty. Somewhere along these lines we may even begin to discover the path that leads from the Great through the Open to the Good Society.

5 Morality, Institutions and Civil Society

Address at the Award Ceremony of the Senator Giovanni Agnelli International Prize, Turin, 30 March 1992

First I want to thank those who have found me worthy of the award of the Agnelli Prize. No other recognition has ever given me greater pleasure. The award bears a name which stands for the best in Italy's tradition of public-spirited entrepreneurs. It is given in the capital of Piedmont in which parliamentary democracy had a home since 1848. The Agnelli Prize also confirms my association with its two previous holders, the moral philosopher, Isaiah Berlin, and the moral economist, Amartya Sen.

I have used the word, *moral*, advisedly, although the Prize is given to emphasize 'the *ethical* dimension in advanced societies'. Somehow I prefer the language of 'morals' to that of 'ethics'. The reason may be idiosyncratic, having to do with the Scottish moral philosophers of the eighteenth century, Adam Smith, Adam Ferguson, with Immanuel Kant's desire to replace 'desolate randomness' by the 'moral whole of society', and with Émile Durkheim's insistence on the 'moral character' of the division of labour as the creator of solidarity. But then, are not *mores* merely the Latin version of the Greek *ethos*? So why worry about the words?

It was Horace who told us – or rather, who told Emperor Augustus in one of his poetic *Epistles* – that the vanquished Greece proceeded to conquer its victor, Rome, in turn, by penetrating its culture in artful ways. Of course such cultural conquests do not leave their perpetrators unchanged; a new blend emerges.

The rest of us Europeans have, I believe, got our civilization from Rome, not from Athens. Virgil, not Homer is the father of the West. Even the dreamy poetess from Lesbos (*phainetai moi kenos isos theoisin*) seems remote by comparison to the jubilant if moody Catullus (*ille mi par esse deo videtur*). While Aristotle matters for the history of science as well as political thought, there is something new, important and lasting in the public thinking of a Cicero and, six centuries later, the jurists of Emperor Justinian. Perhaps, the title of one of their contributions to the teaching of law sums up Rome's gift to the West: *Institutiones*, institutions.

I say this as a native German whose *curriculum vitae* led him at an early age to that modern Rome, Britain, and who returned to the 'blessed isle' time and again until in the end I applied for what is appropriately called, citizenship. A Cambridge professor, Eliza Marian Butler, wrote in the 1930s a brilliant study entitled, *The Tyranny of Greece over Germany*. The study deals with German classical authors and points out that even they were 'inherently romantic' with their 'backward-gazing, dreaming eyes focused on a Greece that never was on sea or land'. The author adds her own 'disturbing' thought which has to do with the capacity of 'the power innate even in the noblest ideas to wreak havoc in real life'. The culprit, to be sure, is 'a Greece that never was'. What is more, Britain has its own romantic and misty fragrances, its Celtic fringe, its Saxon, indeed German ingredients. Yet it is above all the country of John Locke and David Hume, of Adam Smith and Jeremy Bentham, of John Stuart Mill and John Maynard Keynes, that is of eminently practical theorists who did not set out to transform the whole world, let alone to reconstruct an imagined Arcadia, but to improve critical elements of the real conditions of people here and now.

The two British scholars who received the Agnelli Prize before me were born in Latvia and Bengal respectively; I was born in Hamburg. Sir Karl Popper who represents the best of the Roman tradition of Britain was born in Vienna. This century, and notably the Second Thirty Years' War which began when Sir Edward Grey saw 'the lamps go out all over Europe' in August 1914, has tossed us all up, but it has also concentrated the mind. The British Foreign Secretary added at the time: 'and we shall not see them lit again in our lifetime'. He was right of course for himself and his generation, though we, the fortunate survivors, have seen the flicker of lamps re-lit all over Europe; we have lived to see the revolution of 1989. Now, in 1992, the hopes of a new liberty are not unmixed with doubts and fears. The rule of law and the market economy meet with formidable obstacles in the new democracies of Central, Eastern and Southeastern Europe, and it will be a long time yet before they are firmly anchored in civil society. But the light is still there, and for those of us who love freedom above all else, nothing is more important than to shield it against hostile winds and to nourish it so that it can enlighten all Europe and the world beyond.

This then is what my reflections on this occasion are about: morality, institutions, and civil society. Morality tells us what to aim for and what to avoid; it not only inspires decency and humanity in everyday life but also the wish to see life chances spread to all humans, and the actions which flow from this desire. Institutions are the instrument of improvement; at their best, they give reality to the aspirations of the open society, like the institutions of democracy which enable us to elect those by whom we are governed but, more important still, to remove them from office if we feel that they have gone astray. Civil society provides the lifeblood of liberty; its creative chaos of associations gives people the chance to live their lives without having to go begging to the state or to other powers. Perhaps the concept which best sums up all these hopes is the one with which you rightly identified me in the citation for the Agnelli Prize: citizenship.

It would make good sense to reflect on these notions in abstract and draw on historical examples. I hope the occasion will justify that I propose to proceed in a more personal vein and talk about my own discovery of the values of citizenship. Given the times and the circumstances of my life, this will in any case lead to three dates of wider significance: 1945, 1968, 1989.

One of my early publications was a little essay written in 1957 and published under the title, *Homo Sociologicus*. The objective of the essay was twofold. On the one hand, it introduced into German – and in due course, European – sociological discourse the important concept of role. Roles are, in Émile Durkheim's sense, elementary social facts. We enter into social relations not as naked individuals but in the cloaks which our positions in society provide. Somehow we know how to behave as fathers, teachers, members of a club or a party. Expectations surround our positions which acquire an almost separable, indeed separate reality; they can be put into words, taught and learned, observed and violated. If we violate them, there are sanctions to remind us of our duty. *Homo Sociologicus* is man – and woman – the bearer of roles. This familiar thesis would not have made my early essay either exciting or lasting. But I argued something else in it which is that the fact of society is 'vexatious'. *Homo Sociologicus* is an alienated creature. The real, indeed the moral individual can be, and has to be seen apart from all social roles. I used Kant's language to argue that individuals had an 'empirical' and an 'intelligible' character – and the 'intelligible' or moral character has to be encouraged to fight the impositions of man's 'sociological shadow'.

The argument was in part a dialogue with Max Weber. Weber's pre-eminent theme is the desperate and ultimately vain attempt to come to terms with unbearable dichotomies. I can feel with him, for I share his aversion against the great harmonizers, be they of the Rousseauean or the Hegelian variety; but I have also long tried to overcome the theoretical dichotomies by practical propositions. Weber was equally committed to value-free social science and to political reform; but he always insisted that the two must not be confused. 'Science as a vocation' and 'politics as a vocation' are two distinct human endeavours; the politician does not apply science, and the scientist must beware of letting his political convictions intrude on his scholarship. So far, so good. 'The sociologist as such', I said in *Homo Sociologicus* 'is not, and should not be a politician'. But this is not the end of the story, for 'even worse is the sociologist who sees the career of a scientist as requiring him to renounce all critical concern with his own actions and his society'. And thus I took my essay to its rousing conclusion, exhorting the sociologist to 'cease being a brake and become a motor of a society of free men, a society whose vexatiousness, along with the all too passive fantasy of unfilled spaces, is swallowed up in the active reality of freely filled time'.

It is easy to see why many, notably among the young and action-hungry students of the time, liked the approach. Equally, some, notably among the older and experience-scarred scholars, did not. They described my approach as another version of German romanticism, the tyranny of Greece over one young German who dreamt of moral individuals apart from society rather than within it. Helmuth Plessner wrote: 'If in order to make the sphere of freedom unassailable we identify it with that of privacy (and privacy, we should note, in an extra-social sense) freedom loses all contact with reality, all possibility of social realization.' This was not quite my argument, though I did imply that society is never intrinsically moral, and that there is therefore an inevitable conflict between the moral and the social. This conflict cannot be resolved in theory, but it must be resolved in practice. Consequently those who are engaged in the study of society must never neglect their critical function as intellectuals.

Max Weber introduced another distinction, related but different, which is that between an 'ethics of conviction' (*Gesinnungsethik*) and an 'ethics of responsibility' (*Verantwortungsethik*). The former espouses absolute values; it is the morality of saints. The latter recognizes the complexity of means–ends relationships; it is the ethics of politicians. Once again we must ask: is this all? Will the two never meet? Weber died in Year Six of the Second Thirty Years' War which began in 1914 and ended in 1945, so that he was spared the worst of it, Stalin, Hitler. When society took on an absolute or, in the word of Mussolini and later Hitler, a 'total' quality, the ethics of responsibility lost its relevance. Indeed, it became an excuse for that most cowardly of attitudes in our century, collaboration (*Mitläufertum*). 'In order to prevent worse', people who should have known better stayed on and supported regimes for which they were never more than useful idiots. When I was asked by a German newspaper to fill in the famous Proust questionnaire which includes the question 'Which historical figures do you despise most?', I replied without hesitation: 'the cowards, the facilitators who made totalitarianism easy, von Papen in Nazi Germany, Grotewohl in postwar East Germany'. They, or their successors, pose the most difficult questions of public morality in the post-communist countries today.

Insistence on the absoluteness of certain fundamental values was, I believe, the motive of my argument in *Homo Sociologicus*. Never trust authority, for it can be horribly abused! There certainly are conditions – we have seen them prevail in far too many places during this century – in which the 'ethics of conviction' is the only valid morality. Nor does one have to be a saint to espouse it. It is true, active resistance against the temptations of totalitarianism is more than one can demand from others; putting life at risk is a sacrifice which one can only ever demand from oneself. But we have no right ever to compromise with evil. The regimes of China, or Cuba, or Burma are totally unacceptable. Some may have unavoidable dealings with them, but they should not try to camouflage the necessities which motivate them by invoking the 'ethics of responsibility'. Governments which kill and torture, which detain without trial and suppress free speech, challenge our basic values in a manner which allows only one reaction, that is unconditional abhorrence and opposition.

The question is, where to draw the line; for most things in this world are not either black or white. What about contemporary Turkey for example? It is even more difficult to draw the line as one lives through changes which happen slowly and step by step. I shall forever be proud of my father, Gustav Dahrendorf, who knew exactly when, in postwar East Germany, the time had come to say no. He was then Vice-Chairman of the East German Social Democrats, and the issue, on 11 February 1946, was whether to announce to an impending congress of trade unions in Berlin that the Social Democrats were prepared to enter into talks about a possible merger with the Communists. Prepared to enter into talks, no more; many used the argument to shrug their shoulders and acquiesce. But my father knew: *hic Rhodus, hic salta!* His memory of Nazi prisons was still fresh; but he jumped, and once again risked his career and more. He was right. Perhaps we have to rely on some having the sensitivity and the courage to realize when the moment has come at which the cosy world of the 'ethics of responsibility' has to be abandoned and we have to take a stand.

Homo Sociologicus, however, was not written in 1946 in East Berlin, but in 1957, partly in Saarbrücken and partly in Palo Alto in California. There was no question of totalitarian temptations just around the corner in those parts of the world. The 'vexatious fact of society' was therefore taken by many readers to describe the perfectly civil societies of the time, if not society in general. Nor was this a misinterpretation of the text. My attempt to defend myself against Plessner's criticism by reference to David Riesman's 'inner-directed man' and the Anglo-Saxon tradition of the 'minimal state' seems in retrospect somewhat feeble. In fact, many young people felt encouraged to take direct action by the appeal to a moral right to resist society and its impositions altogether. My approach fed into a mood which informed at least some of the protagonists of the turbulent events of 1968.

1968 meant different things in different countries, and it certainly had a different quality in the United States of America, where the Vietnam War and civil rights simultaneously topped the political agenda. On the European continent however, one important thread linking the demonstrations, the wider movement of minds and the specific acts of terrorism – all of which have come to be identified with the year, 1968, though many happened later – was anarchist in intent and anomic in effect; it was a protest against society and its constraints in every shape and form. 'Underneath the gowns, the musty smell of centuries', students chanted and proceeded to demand not (as would have been consistent) that the gowns be cleaned, but that they be abolished altogether and with them the entire structure of university governance. 'Democratization' did not mean the reform of procedures with a view to greater accountability but the removal of all authority in the name of 'unconstrained discourse', the permanent discussion by all of everything.

This is where Jürgen Habermas was liable to be misunderstood until he dissociated himself from those whom he called, the 'fascists of the left'. This is also where Helmuth Plessner was right and I was wrong.

Let me not turn this address into an apology for what I have written in the past, if only to avoid the risk of the Jury withdrawing the Prize which they gave me for my work. There is however a lesson from the experience of 1968 which is relevant for my argument. (I have drawn this lesson in my 1985 Hamlyn Lectures on *Law and Order*.) It is, in a word, that anomy is bad for freedom. The word, anomy, was introduced into modern social science by Durkheim in order to describe a condition which is conducive to suicide. It is a condition of disorientation and disorder. Literally, of course, anomy means the absence of *nomoi*, of laws. In trying to develop a liberal approach to the vexing issues of law and order, I discussed above all the 'no-go areas' of modern societies where prevailing norms do not apply or are not enforced. Some are physical areas; housing estates, subways, streets in large cities. Others are metaphorical areas; youth for example exempts those most likely to break them from social norms. Such 'no-go areas' may well be spreading, and they describe a world in which freedom is turned into the existentialist nightmare in which anything goes and nothing matters. The co-ordinates of meaning and value have crumbled.

In his *Second Treatise of Government*, John Locke offers a wonderfully low-key argument about what he calls, 'the inconveniences of the state of nature'. (Locke was less emotional about it than Hobbes; he was also writing in more auspicious times than the author of the *Leviathan* 40 years earlier.) The state of nature, Locke says, is anarchic and therefore has few benefits. Even the intensely personal relationship of 'conjugal society' or of 'master and servant' do not constitute a basis for civilized life. What is needed is a social contract. 'Those who are united into one body and have a common established law and judicature to appeal to, with authorities to decide controversies between them and punish offenders, are in civil society with one another.' There is a more specific meaning of the concept of civil society; Locke seems to mean little more than 'society' in the sense in which Margaret Thatcher used the word when she made her famous statement: 'There is no such thing as society; there are only individuals – and families.' But Locke's point is clear. If there is no such thing as society, we are right back to the 'inconveniences of the state of nature'. Society protects us from them and it alone gives us our bearings, and it does so by institutions.

Institutions are, as Locke says, in the first instance norms, the sanctions attached to them, and the organizational forms in which these appear; they constitute 'a common established law and judicature to appeal to'. In a somewhat wider sense, these include the accepted mores of living with others, and in a deeper sense, rules have to have meaning. We need not just laws but the 'spirit of laws'. Institutions serve to sustain liberty only if they are not merely 'legal' but also 'legitimate'. Locke is right to add that institutions in this sense always require 'authorities'; the social contract is certainly a 'contract of association', but it is a 'contract of domination' as well. Let me add immediately that I am not referring to just any kind of norms or authorities, though even good societies come in many different shapes and forms. I have in mind rules for which reasons can be given and authorities which are accountable, thus reasonable laws and democratic governments which can be removed and replaced. Other qualifications of the concept of institutions are desirable. For instance, one may wonder how many institutions we need. There may well be a problem of over-institutionalization; of 'hypernomy', as well as one of anomy.

But anomy is the greater worry. It is – if it is not too intrusive for a stranger to say so – Italy's worry. The country in which, admittedly a long time ago, institutions were invented, is now suffering from their weakness. They have to be rebuilt. The absence of effective norms and authorities in the end becomes a threat to liberty. Liberty is neither an original state of man to which we should return by removing all constraints nor a postmodernist void in which anything goes. Liberty is a civilized and civilizing force. It therefore flourishes only if we manage to create and maintain institutions which give it stability and duration. Institutions provide the framework for the provisions from which we choose, including economic prosperity. Institutions guarantee our entitlements, thus social justice. If we want more life chances for more people, we have to work through institutions and must never cease to refine and improve them. In some circumstances, when the risks of anomy grow, the most important single task for the liberal is to build institutions.

It is easy to talk about this task but hard to accomplish it, even under the relatively favourable conditions of Italy in the face of weak government, or the United States in the face of social decomposition. How much harder is it to build institutions when the entire edifice of social order falls apart! This has happened in the formerly communist countries by the revolution of 1989. Some moved more slowly, too slowly perhaps so that the old *nomenklatura* was able to readjust and further dramatic changes are likely; some moved so fast that the resulting vacuum attracted adventurers and speculators rather than institution-builders. Everywhere the social contract itself is at stake, and thus the fundamentals of liberty. At first sight, these are two, political and economic. Democracy and the market economy are the favoured catchwords. In my *Reflections on the Revolution in Europe* I have tried to show how difficult it is to establish even these, and how the conflicting time-scales of political and economic reform threaten the open society. The 'valley of tears' is now all around us.

But even if they succeed, democracy and the market economy are not enough. Liberty needs a third pillar to be safe; its name is, civil society. The whole point of the open society is that our lives take place in associations outside the grasp of the state. Even the public sphere is not primarily political, to say nothing of the economic sphere of activity. The fundamental difference between monopolistic structures such as those of *nomenklatura* socialism and liberal structures is that a plurality of autonomous associations are on offer which are not all geared to one common purpose. Civil society at its best is a creative chaos. It protects us against the 'inconveniences of the state of nature', but also against those arising from monopolistic claims by self-appointed minorities and indeed majorities. To quote James Madison, one of the authors of the *Federalist* papers which prepared the American constitution: civil society is 'broken into so many parts, interests and classes of citizens, that the rights of individuals or of the minority, will be in little danger from the interested combinations of the majority'.

For those who have recently rediscovered their freedom, civil society is a great hope, but it is also hard to appreciate fully. Revolutionary times are highly politicized times. They tear people out of their normal lives; sometimes, unusual figures rise to the top. But this does not last. Suddenly, the author Gabor Kis loses an election within his party; the medieval historian Bronislaw Geremek fails to get a majority in parliament. It is wonderful to see Václav Havel in Prague in the Castle; he more than anyone has found words to describe the new experience of freedom and I shall presently quote him as my witness. Yet civil society will not have been established until Havel can write plays again and criticize his government from outside rather than try to introduce legislation into a parliament which is naturally dominated by more ephemeral forces.

There is an even more serious dimension of civil society which has recently preoccupied me above all. As we watch the struggles of transition in the post-communist world and perhaps try to lend a hand here and there, we cannot fail to be struck by the apparent attraction of all-embracing ideas to those who have just escaped the monopoly of one ideology. They are, it appears, liable to fall for versions of fundamentalism, sometimes religious, more often national or rather tribal, which engender emotions that could, and do, lead to the destruction of liberal institutions. Suddenly, Latvia is more important than liberty, and those who do not belong are made to suffer: minorities, neighbours. Vicious suppression of minorities and civil war spread in many parts of Eastern Europe. History, far from having come to an end, re-emerges in its ugliest form. Why?

There are undoubtedly many and varied reasons. One however seems to me pre-eminent; it has to do with belonging. Democracy and the market economy are fine mechanisms to avoid the entrenchment of errors. They make changes possible which do not hurt unduly. They are eminently reasonable ways of organizing our affairs. But they do not offer people a home. Important human needs remain unsatisfied by the institutions of the open society. Thus people look around elsewhere; and if the going gets rough – elections disappoint, convertibility and privatization do not bring immediate prosperity – people want satisfaction quickly and comprehensively. The hour of false gods has arrived, and that of their worldly spokesmen, the new dictators, as well.

As one observes the violent unfolding of new – and often old – forms of belonging, one appreciates how fortunate those have been who found bonds which do not interfere with liberal political and economic institutions. This was true for America's 'civic religion', the flag next to the bank manager's desk, the frequent invocations of God in worldly affairs; Tocqueville was the first to describe it. It was true also for Swiss citizenship which is that of a canton, and even a small town or village, rather than a diffuse nation-state. The churches, notably when they are established like the Church of England, or quasi-established like the Catholic Church in Ireland, or Poland, or even Italy, have on the whole developed a *modus vivendi* which leaves democracy and the market economy alone, though in the process the ligatures which it offers have come to be weakened. But of course the reverse has happened in Algeria, and it threatens in other parts of the world, including our own if one thinks of the so-called 'Muslim parliament' recently set up in Britain; aggressive creeds take the place of the co-existence of God and Caesar.

If there is any remedy to such threats to liberty at all, it must be in the realm of civil society. The human need for belonging can be satisfied by a plurality of associations which as such have no political claims. There must be strong associations among them which offer bonds at least like those of the Sienese *contrade*, or indeed some political parties in the past, of cohesive small towns and even extended family groups. Without doubt, such strong bonds can in part be replaced and in any case supplemented by a multitude of weaker ones, in working men's clubs, active charities, civic initiatives around particular issues. Business culture is relevant here; companies which promote the pride of belonging make their own contribution to civil society. But as I list examples, the precariousness of this pillar of liberty becomes apparent. It is not only hard to build, it is also liable to crack and crumble, and it ultimately depends as much on the civic sense of individuals as it does on institutions.

But then, liberty needs people who are prepared to fight for it. Václav Havel has proved his mettle, and has also put the objective into words which summarize the argument which I have presented better than I can. In a recent address which he gave in a predominantly Czech community in the United States and which was published under the telling title, *On Home*, Havel said:

I am in favour of a political system based on the citizen, and recognizing all his fundamental civil and human rights in their universal validity, and equally applied: that is, no member of a single race, or single nation, a single sex, or a single religion may be endowed with basic rights that are any different from anyone else's. In other words, I am in favour of what is called a civil society.

And further:

A civil society, based on the universality of human rights, best enables us to realize ourselves as everything we are – not only members of our nation, but members of our family, our community, our region, our church, our professional organization, our political party, our country, our supranational communities – and to be all of this because society treats us chiefly as members of the human race, that is, as people, as particular human beings whose individuality finds its primary, most natural and, at the same time, most universal expression in our status as citizens, in citizenship in the broadest and deepest sense of that word.

The idea of citizenship 'in the broadest and deepest sense of that word' describes the goal of the little journey through the moral education of one European intellectual on which I have taken you. The path 'from subjects to citizens' (to quote Giovanna Zincone's recent book) is the path to freedom. It has to do with morality because citizens have to be civil and civilized. Expressions like civic courage and civic pride are rightly associated with it. The citizen is a proud creature, ready to stand up for basic values of the open society, ready to go to battle for them if need be.

Citizenship is also an institution. This is important. It is not just an attitude of mind, or even a subject of political education, of 'civics' as it used to be called in English schools. Amartya Sen made an important contribution when he focused so much of his thinking about inequality on 'entitlements'. Citizenship is above all a set of entitlements common to all members of society. If there are duties or obligations of citizenship as well, these are in no sense conditions for the rights of citizens. Citizenship rights are those unconditional entitlements which transcend and contain the forces of the market.

I like to think of citizenship as a set of chances – life chances if you wish – which define a free society. The notion is important. The first winner of the Agnelli Prize, Isaiah Berlin, wrote a famous essay on *Two Concepts of Liberty*. He distinguished between what he called 'negative' and 'positive freedom' and expressed a strong preference for the 'negative freedom' from undue constraints whereas he suspected that 'positive freedom' can mislead rulers into prescribing what people have to be or do. I notice that the second winner of the Prize, Amartya Sen, took issue with this thesis, though he accepted the distinction when he argued a brilliant case for both: 'The negative freedoms of newspapers and opposition parties to criticize, publish and agitate can be powerful in safeguarding the elementary positive freedoms of the vulnerable population.' In a recent book of *Conversations with Isaiah Berlin* (by Ramin Jahanbegloo) the author of the distinction actually accepts that both positive and negative freedom raise 'genuine questions; both are inescapable'. I know and accept what he means, which is that the absence of constraints is not enough; people have to be able to make use of the opportunities offered to them. But perhaps this shows the limits of the usefulness of the distinction itself. The point is not that freedom is either negative or positive, but that it is a chance – a condition in which people are in a position to choose their own way both in the sense of no one preventing them and of their being enabled to do so. No one should be made to take a particular choice or even be guided towards it; freedom includes the options not to choose at all or to choose wrongly. But those for whom choice remains a cynical promise without any reality, are not free. Negative freedom can become the freedom of the few to enrich themselves without bounds; freedom as chance is not only general, but above all, real.

Citizenship epitomizes liberty in this sense. Civil society is the medium in which it thrives. In civil society the citizen is at home. Liberals sometimes risk being unduly concerned with means rather than ends, with democratic institutions and markets rather than human well-being. To some extent this is as it should be; in a free society people are not told how to live their lives, they are even allowed to be unhappy. But citizenship and civil society go one important step further than elections and markets. They are goals to strive for rather than dangers to avoid. In this sense they are moral objectives, which is why I want to commend them to your attention and care.

6 Why Excellence Matters

*Keynote Address on the occasion of the conferment of the Prix Latsis
Universitaires at the University of Geneva, 2 November 1995*

It is a pleasure to congratulate the winners of the Latsis Prize on the just reward
for their remarkable achievements. It is always a pleasure to see excellence
recognized. We rejoice with those who are obviously delighted with their
awards. We are also glad that such individuals exist, outstanding people who
set an example to which others can aspire.

But in this democratic age this is already a controversial statement which
takes me to the heart of the subject of my remarks. Excellence has got a bad
name; one almost has to apologize for it. Certainly the British Arts Council
had to offer lengthy explanations for giving the bulk of the money which it
distributes to the Royal Opera House at Covent Garden and the Sadler's Wells
theatre. Why did London get so much and Liverpool so little? The University
of Oxford has to explain why many of its new entrants come from a limited
number of top schools. How can we justify the privilege? There is even a
tendency to award prizes not to individuals but to deserving yet anonymous
groups or organizations – to Amnesty, to Pugwash – in order to avoid
elevating individuals to hero's status. I am going to argue that this is not only
mistaken, but dangerously wrong, and that excellence matters, for all of us.

What though is excellence? Vilfredo Pareto has had a go at this vexing
question in the famous §2027 of his *Traité de Sociologie Générale*. Let us
give marks (he argues) to people's capacity in all branches of human activity,
10 for the best, zero for the worst. Thus the successful professional gets a
10, one who has no clients a 1, and he who is *vraiment crétin* a zero. 'He
who has made millions, whether by fair means or foul, is given a 10. He who
has made thousands is given a 6. He who just about manages to survive, is
given a 1, and those who end up in the poorhouse a zero.' Pareto proceeds
to the *femmes politiques,* to Perikles's Aspasia, the Maintenon of Louis
XIV, the Pompadour of Louis XV, who get, interestingly, not a 10, but an
8 or 9 for having captured the affection of a great man and influenced the
ways in which he governs. The whore, on the other hand, who merely
satisfies the senses of men and has no influence on public affairs, must
make do with a zero. And so on, to the great crook who gets away with murder
and the small one who is caught by the police, the great poet and the miserable
rhymer, the grandmaster of chess and the hopeless amateur. In this way Pareto
wants to constitute a whole class of tens, as it were, of those who excel in

61

their branches, a 'select class' for which he introduces that other word which is never far away as one speaks of excellence, *elite*.

Two questions at least remain. One is: do we really want to lump the Pompadour, Goethe, George Soros and Gary Kasparow together in one elite which would have to include other, much less savoury characters as well? Probably not. Some public, even moral relevance has to be added to sheer achievement. The other question is: who gives the marks, the tens and the noughts? Pareto rightly observes that in chess one can count the number of games won or lost, but not in poetry, science or politics. An element of judgement enters here. Whose judgement? Who is the jury? Those who have awarded the Latsis Prize will be well aware of the agony of decision. In the end, as in the case of trial juries, we rely on the common sense of people. However, whereas trial juries can and must be based on the simple common sense of citizens, judgements of excellence require a groomed common sense; they have to be informed judgements. This is where peer review comes in, with all the dangers of trade unionization of peer groups and indeed mutual backscratching which it involves.

Having raised the questions, I shall assume that we know the answers: there is such a phenomenon as publicly and morally relevant excellence, and we know how to identify it. Why does it matter?

The case which I want to put to you rests on a line of argument which begins with the thesis that equality alone is stifling and ultimately deadly. Note that I said, equality *alone*. The basic entitlements of citizenship for all are an indispensable condition of civilized and liberal communities. Indeed, exclusion from these entitlements is one of the major social problems of the 1990s, not just on a world scale but within even the most advanced countries. This is the problem of the underclass, and also that of xenophobia. Inclusion involves basic rights, equality before the law, due process, the integrity of the person, freedom of expression and association. It also involves chances of participation, universal suffrage, of course, but equally importantly market access including labour market access, and social involvement in the numerous opportunities of civil society. This is what we mean by citizenship in the full sense of the word.

It can also be called, equality of opportunity. But such equality is only one half of the life chances which people seek and deserve. The other half has to do with the opportunities themselves. Freedom of expression is almost meaningless if there is only one newspaper or television station; it is severely restricted also if most newspapers and television stations are owned and run by the same proprietor, public or private. The variety needed for life chances is, moreover, not just lateral, a plurality of intrinsically similar provisions. It is also scalar, a diversity of levels, of ranks, a world in which some have more of what people value than others. This is, of course, the crux of the argument: is citizenship compatible with inequality? Or, in the words of the education debate: can we be equal and excellent too?

The answer is not simple and must not be facile; it is, nevertheless, yes. There are two limiting conditions which make inequality unacceptable. Both have been mentioned already. One is exclusion from the universe of opportunity. Where this occurs, action is needed in the interest of a civilized and liberal community. The existence of an underclass destroys the moral texture of societies. At the other end of the scale, it is not acceptable that anyone occupies a position of such power that he or she can deny others the exercise of their citizenship rights. This is meant by privilege in the strict sense of the term. Privilege by birth or arrogation denies the universality of citizenship. Some remnants of such privilege still exist; strong forces in all three British political parties want to abolish voting rights for hereditary peers in the House of Lords (though they may not have chosen the most flagrant case of privilege). More importantly today, control of unaccountable instruments of power, notably though by no means only the media, raises serious issues.

Within the limits thus set, that is, in the absence of exclusion on the one hand, and privilege or concentrations of private power on the other, inequality is not only compatible with citizenship, but highly desirable. Entitlements are barren without provisions, opportunities empty without a range of possible outcomes. In that sense, the American Dream embodied a perfect vision of a free society, even if reality never fully lived up to it and perhaps (as Tocqueville first argued) could not live up to it: 'They have swept away the privileges of some of their fellow creatures which stood in their way, but they have opened the door to universal competition.' 'But'? Or could it after all be, 'and'? Competition within rules is not the worst prescription for enhancing the life chances of the greatest number.

It is easy to see that competition benefits those who succeed. Tocqueville argued that it also makes the losers envious and restless. Robert Merton made this conflict between cultural values and social capacities the central plank of his 'Social Structure and Anomie' and spoke of an inherent 'strain towards anomie'. What then is the answer? For Tocqueville it is the nostalgia for an age of aristocracy: 'When inequality of conditions is the common law of society, the most marked inequalities do not strike the eye; when everything is nearly on the same level, the slightest [inequalities] are marked enough to hurt it.' Tocqueville was no fool; he knew that the French Revolution could not be undone. His conclusion is thus gloomy. What he wants, is forever gone, what has come in its place, is not viable. A century and a half after *Democracy in America* we know that the gloom was exaggerated if not unwarranted.

Robert Okun has plausibly argued (in his *Equality and Efficiency*) that government-created inequalities are much more drastic than those arising from competitive markets. In any case, competition by rules can be a highly creative process, its highly unequal outcomes notwithstanding. The American dream was real for a long time, even if it is under threat today, when for the first time in the history of the country the majority of parents have to tell their children that they are going to be worse off than they, the parents, were.

Inequality is not the same as excellence, but where excellence is recognized, it is accepted that equality of opportunity must not mean equality of outcomes. This leaves the question still unanswered, what – apart from the intrinsic satisfaction for those who are given a Pareto ten,and a prize to go with it – is so good about excellence? I want to cite two such desirable effects.

The first is innovation. Stagnant societies – stagnant economies and polities – are precarious societies. The American economist Mancur Olson has described the risk strikingly in his *Rise and Decline of Nations*. He quotes Pandit Nehru: 'Every civilization which resists change declines.' He could have quoted Immanuel Kant, who built his 'Idea of a General History with Cosmopolitan Intent' on the notion that while people dream of a forever tranquil Arcadia, they have fortunately not been made for it; conflict and competition drive them on to new horizons. But a tendency towards entropy remains. Stagnation, even stagflation; 'distributional coalitions'; vested interests; the desire for protection; guilds and trade unions; bureaucracy and other rigidities recur. They all serve to cement a stagnant mediocrity. Remember the word, 'Eurosclerosis'?

It did not last. Europe is not alone in the world, and when the dragons and tigers elsewhere set about their predatory endeavours, the challenge was clear. Some rose to it. They were Schumpeter-type entrepreneurs with their 'creative destructiveness'. They were also politicians, like Ronald Reagan or Margaret Thatcher, or on the European scene, Jacques Delors. Some of the names show that the innovators are not necessarily the most likeable figures. The same is true for excellence in general. Whoever stands out not only provokes envy but is also likely to have traits which are less useful in making friends than in making headway. Arcadia is in a certain sense nicer than the open society. But it is (in Kant's words) a place for sheep rather than human beings, or (in Popper's words) for tribes rather than enlightened citizens.

Innovation requires outstanding deeds, inventions, their translation into reality, that is entrepreneurialism, the acceptance of the needs of leadership, thus excellence of one kind or another. It helps us break out of the 'iron cage of bondage' of modern bureaucratized states. It also does something else which takes me to the second desirable effect of excellence which I wanted to cite. It sets the tone.

Here we enter a minefield of controversy, at least in a politically correct world. There is, in modern societies, not only the risk of levelling, of stagnant mediocrity, but also an air of disorientation. This too can be the result of a misguided concept of democracy. Values are thought to 'emerge' somehow, by freeing people from constraints, encouraging them to be their best selves, bringing them together for discourse and communication. Somehow, like geysers out of Icelandic soil, truth and goodness and beauty will arise. This is Habermas (albeit in caricature), and Rousseau before him. But it is wrong. Values do not just emerge, not even from unconstrained discourse. We have all experienced committees in search of a big idea. It does not just come; somebody has to have it. Somebody even has to try to persuade others of it, and persuasion is bound to be a mixture of argument, marketing skills and power, in other words more than just a rational process.

Paul Feyerabend first elevated the notion that 'anything goes' to a theory of knowledge. The ironic anarchist of method knew, more or less, what he was doing. What he may not have known is the extent to which the erosion of standards, and of the readiness to set standards, has in fact taken place. Mixing modern medicine with acupuncture, Oriental potions and a bit of magic is one of the more harmless results. Making what most people would still call, reality, disappear by interpretation into a multitude of virtual realities is a rather more serious phenomenon. Taking a 'why not?' approach to whatever people do, say, want, and look like is a step towards anomy, the absence of rules. Anomy, however, like entropy, is ultimately death, Hobbes's war of all against all in the case of anomy, Rousseau's Arcadia of human sheep without memory or purpose in the case of entropy.

Somebody has to set the tone so that all of us have standards by which to measure quality, and even against which to assert alternatives. (If anything goes, all debate and dispute ceases, along with all meaning.) You will begin to wonder whether a died-in-the-wool liberal is turning into an authoritarian. I hope that in my final remarks I can persuade you that this is not the case; on the contrary, it is Arcadia and the war of all against all which invite warlords and dictators. Liberty requires institutions and conflict, a tone that is set and the opportunity to dispute it, it requires a society open for change rather than rigidity or meaningless multitude.

Setting the tone has much to do with excellence. If I was chairman of the Arts Council I would neither apologize for having given so much money to Covent Garden and Sadler's Wells, nor promise that sooner or later provincial opera houses and theatre companies will get funds of a similar order of magnitude. I would argue that it is important for all that the very best flourish, because without them all would soon lose their bearings. This is true for universities too. In the classless society which Conservative governments in Britain have first created and then openly advocated, Oxford and Cambridge are under growing pressure. Why should students get higher grants to attend the ancient universities? Because these are setting the tone for the rest, and a tone which has meant that until recently, the whole British university system was better than the sad 'mass transit system' into which most continental universities have deteriorated. It is true that not everyone can have the best, but even those who get less than the best will be better served when the best is there to see. Take away excellence and you get not only mediocrity everywhere, but worse still, complacent mediocrity.

Are there then no problems with excellence at all? There are, and I must not conclude without highlighting them. Pareto, having devised the wonderful department-store notion of an elite of the 'tens' of all walks of life, states without much ado that he now wants to divide the lot into two: 'We single out those who directly or indirectly play a notable role in government; they constitute the governing elite. The rest will form the non-governmental elite.' This is then a ruling class of those who are given a ten for ... well, for what? And by whom? To be sure, we want to be governed well. There is also much to be said for having a political class with certain standards and even a certain cohesion (though that is another argument, and one which leads us even more deeply into controversy). But beyond that, Pareto's definitions demand words of caution rather than support. One word of caution is that power must never rest on the qualities of individuals. However excellent people are, it is more important that we make sure that they cannot lead us astray than that we give them a free run. This is where an institutional concept of democracy comes into its own. Democracy is about being able to get rid of governments without bloodshed. It may even justify a '22nd Amendment' by which a President cannot be re-elected more than once. In other words, setting the tone is never a justification for keeping a particular person or party in power unchecked and over long periods of time. The whole point of my argument is that change is the lifeblood of liberty.

This, of course, is pure Popper, and so is another comment. I left the question open, for what capacities or achievements the ruling elites in Pareto's sense get their tens. Using his terminology, it has got to be clear that a ten in a non-governing activity cannot and must not be thought of as a qualification for government. Popper's vicious critique of Plato's notion of philosopher-kings remains valid. 'The sage whose magical powers raise him high above ordinary men' is a tyrant who cannot be removed because he has a claim to truth. He must not happen, or even she! A Nobel Prize does not give its laureate a special claim to wisdom in public affairs, nor does outstanding success in business, or even in acting on the stage or the screen. There are scientist-politicians, businesspeople-politicians, even actor-politicians, but their past professions are biographical facts, not sources of legitimate power. This source is in the constitution of liberty, and whether they discharge their duties well will be measured more by Socratic than by Platonic standards. To quote Popper again: Socrates 'warned the statesman against the danger of being dazzled by his own power, excellence and wisdom, and [...] tried to teach him what matters most – that we are all frail human beings'.

Excellence matters. It contributes to keeping societies open and capable of change. It provides innovation and sets standards. By extending the range of choices and offering a sense of direction it contributes to enhancing the life chances of all. At the same time, identifying and praising excellence runs counter to important trends of our world. The question is therefore how we can preserve and develop opportunities for excellence. I am not even going to try and delve into this complicated issue; but I am sure that a prize like the one awarded today is itself an excellent example of how to promote excellence.

7 Prosperity, Civility and Liberty: Can We Square the Circle?

Thank-Offering to Britain Fund Lecture given at the British Academy, London, 12 March 1996. An adapted and amended version was given as the Horowitz Memorial Lecture at the Davis Institute, Hebrew University of Jerusalem, on 22 December 1996

The Jewish refugees whose generous thank-offering to Britain led, along with a research fellowship, to this series of lectures, knew what they were grateful for. It was their survival, of course, but it was more, a new life in a free and civil country. Britain did not have 'the best constitution ever written' as that of Weimar Germany has been described (which Hitler tore up in one short session of the Reichstag on 23 March 1933); Britain did – and does – not have a written constitution at all; yet no one who came to this country as a refugee from persecution in the 1930s ever doubted that he or she was safe from arbitrary rule and protected by institutions, as well as deeply engrained habits, which an unbroken tradition had made more reliable than any Basic Law or Constitutional Court can guarantee.

I came to this country not as a refugee but as one who wanted to make this his home, and thus I have, in a different way, every reason to be grateful to those who received me with such generosity. What is it that attracted a German who had spent more than half his adult life outside Germany when he came in 1974 but who had also been deeply involved in German academic and public affairs? Liberty certainly had something to do with it. There is a quality of freedom which is more than elections and parliamentary debates and incorruptible judges and the chance to write a letter to an editor or even to stand on a crate at Speakers' Corner and harangue the bystanders. I suppose it has something to do with the absence of the ominous black cloud of doubt, even fear, which overshadows so much of life in other countries because it reminds people of violent storms of the past. It is the track record of the country, and notably the sense that whatever illiberal sentiments creep into debate and behaviour, at the end of the day people will not allow the destruction of the liberal order to happen.

Then there is something else. Even the title of this lecture – to say nothing of my other publications – betrays my penchant for the family of words, indeed

68

of ideas and institutions, associated with the city: citizenship, civilization, civic sense and civic virtues, civil society, civility. Curiously, these words are not often used in British parlance. I remember a party leader saying to me: 'Unlike President Mitterrand I cannot go on television and start by addressing my audience as "Citizens and ..." and what, anyway?' (I later discovered in the *Oxford Dictionary* that there is actually an obsolete word, *citizette*.) Civil society is a concept more often used in the post-communist countries of East Central Europe than here. Perhaps awareness for the values of civilized living in civic communities has grown in recent years; there is now a Citizenship Trust; civic sense is mobilized for initiatives, notably at the local level; civil society may yet come to compete with the stakeholder society for the hearts and minds of voters. Could it be that the words become more current as the values behind them seem to retreat? Is the discovery of citizenship, of civil society, of civic sense and civil behaviour a response to the experience of disintegration, to widespread anti-social behaviour and to the crude competition between individuals embodied in the 'philosophy' of *Enrichissez-vous, Messieurs*?

You will notice that I have not yet mentioned prosperity; yet in some ways it is at the heart of my argument. To be sure, many recent refugees have come to Britain for its relative prosperity as much as its liberty and civility. But while wealth creation has preoccupied businessmen and politicians in this country for over a century now – ever since those obsessed with league tables observed that Britain was about to be overtaken by others – somehow not much was done about it. Beveridge, even Keynes, were the heroes and both were as concerned about social cohesion as about wealth creation. Britain may have started it all, with the industrial revolution, but having done so it soon indulged in the dream of an 'English Culture' that can survive the 'decline of the industrial spirit' and in this way even represents a 'future that works' (to allude to the titles of two then much-quoted books of the 1970s by Martin Wiener and by Robert Nossiter).

The last 15 years have swept such nostalgia away. Two great changes happened, not out of the blue, nor only through the deliberate action of governments, yet they came as a surprise, and they were certainly reinforced by political leaders. One is a great leap into modernity at the expense of all remaining traditional institutions; the other is a profound change of language, and more, from that of public-spirited, and often public-sector institutions, to that of business. Suddenly, the much-maligned and arguably least successful profession in the country, that of businessmen and managers, was given prime position and direct responsibility even for public institutions, hospitals and prisons, schools and research councils. In fact, both transformations, that of modernity and that of economism can be seen as the late, the very late triumph of the middle classes in a country which was dominated by upper-class and working-class values longer than any comparable society.

The implications of this change are vast, though I cannot dwell on them in the present context. When I wrote my little popular tract *On Britain* 15 years ago, I pointed to the ambivalence of social values and structures. Strengths in one respect are weaknesses in another, and vice versa. Britain's civility may not have been good for business, but the exclusive emphasis on prosperity has dented a great tradition of civility. Do we have to make a choice? Insofar as lectures have a purpose beyond edification and entertainment, this one is intended to explore ways of having the best of all worlds, of squaring the circle of prosperity, civility and liberty.

This is not a British problem alone, though here it arises from a peculiar angle. The problem is as world-wide as the process of economic internationalization which has followed the information revolution and the globalization of financial markets. When I first wrote about it, the resulting paper was presented to a fringe meeting of the Copenhagen Summit on Social Development. A translated version of that paper has been in the top six of the Italian bestseller lists – non-fiction, I should add – for more than six months. At the same time the founder of the American Communitarian movement, Amitai Etzioni, gave it prominence in his journal *The Responsive Community*. The thesis also formed the background of the work of the Commission on Wealth Creation and Social Cohesion which I had the pleasure to chair. Its report was recently debated in the House of Lords, and I have spoken about it on more than one occasion.

The core thesis is simple. Internationalized modern economies pose a social and political dilemma. In free societies, the search for competitiveness seems to damage social cohesion. If, on the other hand, such free societies choose to give social cohesion a higher priority, their competitiveness, and with it their prosperity, are at risk. Some countries, or at least their leaders, insist on competitiveness but do not want to sacrifice social cohesion and seem to achieve this by restricting political freedom. More and more people think that you can have two but not all three: prosperity and cohesion without freedom, prosperity and freedom without civility, civility and freedom without prosperity. What would need to be done to square the circle?

The thesis sounds abstract but is in fact very close to the experience of many. To prove the point, the rest of my lecture is the tale of three cities, in different parts of the world, admittedly unequal in size but each in its way a part of the story that needs to be told. To the three I shall then add a sketch of a fourth, not exactly a city on the hill, but one that approximates the unachievable and nearly squares the circle of prosperity, civility and liberty.

The first city is a small town in the Middle West of the United States of America. Twenty years ago, the engine manufacturer was at the heart of the lives of its 40 000 or so inhabitants. Most of them were directly or indirectly employed by the company. The local hospital thrived on company-supported health schemes. The local college benefited from direct donations and of course the ability of well-paid parents to pay fees for their children's studies. Famous architects were invited by the company to design public buildings. Sports teams and amateur orchestras, school trips and retirement parties and much else, including a well-known French chef to please the palates of visitors, all owed their wherewithal to the company.

Then the winds of internationalization hit the happy township with gale force. In two waves, several thousand employees were made redundant. Many of them found other jobs – we are, one must remember, in America – but these were, and are, jobs at half the previous income and without any of the old perks. The hospital closed most of its specialist departments; the college lost its standing with its distinguished teachers; what is left of fun and games is no longer public and communal but has withdrawn to the virtual reality of television. The company is still competitive and successful, but the town is a sad shadow of its former self.

The example may sound a little too neat to be true; my friend, the chairman and chief executive of the company, would probably say that I overstated the change; moreover, the example is that of a one-factory town, and such towns have always been vulnerable. Also, American examples are unique in that they are set in a cultural environment unlike others, unlike in particular that of Britain. The capacity for job creation is but one relevant difference; the strength of civil society, and corresponding weakness of central government, is another. Yet when all is said and done, the city tells the Anglo-American story of the last 15 years.

Turning to Britain, the emphasis of public policy was on creating conditions of competitive growth and encouraging entrepreneurs from both home and abroad to make use of this environment. The contribution of public policy to this end followed almost IMF-style recipes (or were these recipes borrowed from the American experience in the first place?): (relatively) low direct taxation, (relatively) low non-wage labour cost, greater labour market flexibility, low entry cost for new companies, deregulation, privatization of state enterprises, in a word, the withdrawal of the state from the economic playing field. This environment allowed companies to become leaner and perhaps fitter; it opened the door to experimentation with allegedly optimal company sizes; it encouraged inward investment. Compared with those who took another route, the performance of the British economy in these 15 years may not have been astounding; there certainly was no economic miracle; but Britain did better than was to be expected on past performance.

All this, moreover, was achieved under the auspices of elected governments and with the support of Parliament. Whatever the constitutional issues which have become a part of public debate may be, and however much Charter 88 and others may worry about civil liberties and democratic institutions, there can be little doubt that the constitution of liberty is basically alive and well in Britain.

If there is another side to the picture, it is social, and this is serious. Its most telling expression is the fact that in the mid-1990s, GNP growth is no longer an indicator of people's well-being. While governments still triumphantly produce macroeconomic statistics, voters feel that something has gone wrong, or at least not gone right. The very concept of wealth has become an issue. (It has been that in the United States for some time, at least since Robert Reich, President Clinton's first Labour Secretary, put it into the stark words that for the first time in American history parents have to tell their children that they will not be as well off as they, the parents, are.) Wealth, in the full sense of Adam Smith's use of the word, or better still, well-being is obviously not a direct result of competitiveness.

The reasons for this disjunction are many. One is that the class which expected to be the harbinger of a better future, the middle class, is the main victim of the new competitiveness thrust. From (very) early retirement, if not outright redundancy, to a flagging housing market, middle-class disenchantment has many causes and facets. They even include the reduced services of the welfare state which paradoxically – some would say, perversely – always benefited the middle classes as much as the poor. Another reason why competitiveness does not produce happiness is the weakening of stakeholder relationships in favour of the cruder cash nexus of shareholders who can buy and sell their interest all too easily. The diminishing role of local communities tells the story most dramatically.

Looking at the wider society, the most serious effect of a leaner and fitter economy is the new exclusion of large social groups. This takes a number of forms. One is lateral exclusion, or with a more drastic word, xenophobia. Frightened citizens do not like strangers. Another form of exclusion is the new poverty. It is now widely recognized that flexibility, especially labour market flexibility, has side effects. It may well be that the most flexible economies create more jobs than the rigid ones, but a significant number of these jobs are so low-paid that they leave their holders unable to sustain a decent standard of living. The figures produced by the Rowntree Trust about growing inequalities are most significant with respect to the absolute position of poverty among the lowest paid 20 per cent. In addition, there is the underclass of those who have lost all hope of being a part of the labour market, the political community, civil society. Some say that as many as 10 per cent have dropped to this status. The figure of 20 plus 10 would tally with the 40:30:30 society described by Will Hutton in his book, *The State We're In*: 40 per cent fairly secure middle class, 30 per cent in a precarious and shifting condition, 30 per cent excluded in one way or another.

The precise figures are important but they are not the main point of the argument. Nor is the threat of revolution the point. The excluded will not start a new revolutionary movement. The problem is, in the most serious sense of the word, moral. A society which claims to be civil but tolerates the exclusion of significant numbers from its opportunities, has betrayed the values on which it is based. The citizens of such a society cannot be surprised if its values are flaunted not just by the excluded themselves but by anyone who sees what is going on, and notably by the young. This is where the link between social exclusion and threats to law and order becomes apparent. It is not that the long-term unemployed, let alone the single mothers of the underclass, are the main perpetrators of crime (their main offence is for the most part to defraud an ineffectual social security system); the point is that the existence of such groups encourages others to ignore and then violate the civic values which are apparently no longer taken seriously.

The combination of greedy individualism and new exclusion is a high price to pay for macroeconomic success in a free society. Britain's major partners in continental Europe are as yet not ready to pay the price. They cling to what is variously called, *économie sociale* or *soziale Marktwirtschaft*, to a social market economy. In France or Germany or Italy, as in Britain, the constitution of liberty is an accepted framework. Democracy and the rule of law may not be as firmly anchored as in the Anglo-Saxon world, and may even have another meaning for many, but they are by and large beyond dispute. The difference is in the relative weight given to economic and social factors of well-being.

Another city comes to mind, somewhat larger than the one-factory town which I described earlier, and in Italy. While not a one-factory town, the beautiful place is basically a one-industry town. One way or another, everyone is connected with food processing, including the production of machines for the purpose. The town is closely linked to its surrounding countryside where much of the food for processing is produced. It is justly proud of the quality of its products. But more, its economic community is as close-knit as its social and political texture. If any one of the dozens of small and medium-sized companies is in trouble, the others will help. Enthusiasm for the local football club is general, especially since at one point it became a contender for the national championship. The local radio and television station, as well as the leading newspaper, are owned by the industrialists' association. The companies also sustain a theatre, a gallery. People naturally like good eating for which the city is famous. It is indeed the envy of many.

And competitiveness? Global markets? Just recently, a trace of fear has crept into the European city. At first, confident producers would not believe that cheaper 'imitation' products could sweep the market; but when the first supermarket began to sell them outside the city boundaries, they began to wonder. Of course they believe that their tomato concentrate is better than tomato ketchup (of which there may soon be a synthetic variety); but young people will insist on covering everything they eat in cheap ketchup and not ever buy what our civic entrepreneurs regard as the real thing. Whatever textbooks say, quality does not always win in the global marketplace. Moreover, contrary to their peers in the French province of Champagne, people failed to patent the name of the city as a brand name; suddenly, 'their' products appear from all over the European Union and beyond. Even the largest of the many companies begins to worry. To make matters worse, the local football club now finds itself in the relegation zone. And so this apparently healthy and happy town runs into the problems which we can now observe all over the European continent.

The profound differences in economic culture between Britain and its European partners are often underrated. Despite the fact that the winds of globalization are common to all, these differences are unlikely to go away. Companies on the continent are for the most part not simply profit machines for shareholders; even in published statistics, turnover is regarded as more significant than profit or market capitalization. Companies are even ranked by the number of people they employ, the implication being that high employment marks a positive contribution to the social economy. As a result – or as a part of the same syndrome – people saw no particular problem in high taxes, high non-wage labour cost, a well-financed welfare state, low labour mobility. For many, a pay-as-you-go pension system, or as Germans prefer to call it, a 'contract between generations' is maintained by which today's workers pay for yesterday's and pensions are therefore not funded. This may well be the key difference between economic cultures, and also the one which raises the largest questions at a time at which the working population is shrinking and the retired population is growing apace.

For not only is the second city of my tale beginning to worry, the entire social market economy of continental Europe is under strain. Sweden's transformation in recent years has been commented on by many. A country which used to have no unemployment and a cradle-to-grave welfare state (as well as prohibitive taxes which drove many of the most successful abroad) has undergone a dramatic transformation. In fact, this was, and is, traumatic as much as dramatic, for it touches the core of Sweden's self-image and national pride. Many think that Germany will have to go down the same road. There are certainly indications: large-scale redundancies in major companies; a serious debate about the attractiveness, or otherwise, of Germany for business; massive cuts in public expenditure; increasing individual contributions to welfare state services. The list is long, and familiar, and the issues dominate public and political debate.

However, there is little reason for *Schadenfreude* on the part of those who have been through the purgatory of competitiveness already. The main themes of socio-economic policy making are very different in Britain and in, say, Germany. (It must be noted in passing that this does not exactly help European integration.) But it would be wrong to assume that as each country tackles its own perils, we are all eventually moving to the same destination. Economic cultures run as deep as the cultures of language and literature, or of governance. There may be a certain degree of convergence but despite exposure to the same winds of internationalization, pension systems, levels of taxation, welfare arrangements, the role of stakeholders, of local communities, and even the structure of firms will remain very different in the English-speaking countries from those who speak French or German or Italian or Spanish. It may be that the new democracies of East Central Europe will find that their dream of emulating the social market economies cannot be realized for lack of resources, and that they will have to move therefore in the Anglo-Saxon direction. One country, the Czech Republic, has already done so. In any case, a true convergence of economic culture in Europe is very unlikely for a long time to come.

East Central Europe of course is not just faced with the alternative of individualistic Anglo-Saxon competitiveness and the social market economy. There is a third mode of combining economic, social and political factors, a third city as it were. It is beyond doubt competitive, indeed it is often held up as a model for economic success in internationalizing markets. But competitiveness and increasing prosperity is not all. The third city – larger than the other two, and in Asia – also places great emphasis on social cohesion. It actually has public policies explicitly designed 'to promote social cohesiveness'. One central element of these policies is a gigantic organization which provides people with housing. More than 80 per cent of the population come under its control. People have to buy their apartments though they cannot sell them without permission. Moreover, the housing agency places them in estates in which the various ethnic groups of the city are represented in proportion to their strength. Once resident in their housing estate people assume a number of obligations to look after others, and they are themselves looked after in case of need.

The organization of housing is only a part of a comprehensive system of state-backed social control. Young people are guided through the educational system in accordance with their assessed abilities. If they make it to a university degree they are even likely to be sent out to sea for cruises on 'love boats' with graduates of the other sex, in the expectation that they will breed a new generation of graduates. (Echoes of the eugenics debate among Fabians and other early social engineers a century ago?) The state determines not only in general terms but often in detail how people are to behave. They must not chew gum or throw away cigarette ends, for example. Such laws are enforced rigorously. Even minor trespasses are punished by caning or prison sentences.

And of course this paradise without crime or unemployment, without eccentrics or dissidents, is also a place in which political life is strictly regulated. The local papers report much about the evils of the rest of the world but only government pronouncements from home. Foreign papers are allowed in as long as they are compliant; if not, they are banned or sued. Those locals who tried to stand for opposition parties – and in two or three cases were actually elected to parliament – soon found their activities severely curtailed, if not cut short by trumped-up charges which ended them in prison.

This is the 'Asia that can say no' (to quote the prime minister of a state neighbouring on my third city). It is competitive and cohesive but certainly not free. It is, in the terms of political science, authoritarian. Authoritarian does not mean totalitarian; as long as people do their own thing, abide by the laws and abstain from meddling in public affairs, they are left unmolested. The temptation of such authoritarianism is not confined to Asia. I mentioned East Central Europe. The return of former communists to political power is at least in part due to the nostalgia of elderly voters for the orderly world of late communism with its full employment, institutionalized child care, secure if modest housing at low rents, complete welfare services, and the famous 'niches' of privacy in which people were allowed to enjoy their 'inner freedom' as long as they did not produce *samizdat* papers or support priests who refused to become poodles of the *nomenklatura*.

What is more, the temptation of authoritarianism is now widespread in the West. I have a growing file of utterances by Western businessmen and politicians, intellectuals and newspaper tycoons, which sound for example like this:

Singapore is not liberal but clean and free of drug addicts. Not so long ago it was an impoverished, exploited colony with hunger, disease and other problems. Now people find themselves in three-bedroom apartments, with jobs and well-cleaned streets. Countries like Singapore take the right way forward.

Those who offered their thanks to Britain when it gave them shelter will remember similar descriptions of Nazi Germany at the time of the 1936 Olympics, and of course Mussolini's promise to make Italian trains run on time. This is not to say that authoritarianism is bound to lead to totalitarianism. On the contrary, while totalitarianism is inherently catastrophic and therefore unstable, authoritarian government can last for a long time. A new authoritarianism may indeed be the main challenge to liberal democracy in the decades to come. If we are prosperous and secure, why worry about liberty?

The answer is that liberty is untidy and complex, it is full of disunity and conflict, it demands activity rather than allowing passive withdrawal, but it is the only condition which enables us to be our best selves and enhance the life chances of all. Karl Popper has put this well in his peroration on the open society: 'If we wish to remain human,' he said, 'we must go on into the unknown, the uncertain and insecure, using what reason we may have to plan for both security *and* freedom'. Long before Popper, Immanuel Kant in his 'Idea for a Universal History with Cosmopolitan Intent' had mocked man's dream of an Arcadia in which 'people, good-natured like the sheep in their pastures, would give their existence no greater value than their animal flocks have'. Fortunately (thus Kant) 'nature' has endowed humans with contradictions, and notably with that of 'unsocial sociability'. Humans want peace and quiet but nature knows better what is good for them, it wants conflict and change. This is what liberty means. How do we bring it about? By creating, says Kant, a 'civil society within the rule of law'.

This is a British Academy lecture, not a parliamentary speech or even an address to a fringe meeting of the United Nations. I feel free, therefore, to end with principles rather than policy prescriptions. Not that it would be difficult to present such prescriptions. They would range from incentives for long-term investment to reforms of the welfare state, from a new approach to education based on individual learning accounts to an improvement of economic reporting by a wealth audit. However, behind such specific policy proposals there is the search for an application of Kant's vision and Popper's moral imperative to contemporary Europe, and to Britain within it.

The key to squaring the circle is strengthening, and in part rebuilding civil society. This is notably the task in Britain where much has been done to enhance economic competitiveness, and democratic institutions are still strong. By civil society I mean that texture of our lives with others which does not need governments to sustain it because it is created by grass-root initiatives. Tocqueville called it democracy, though the institutional connotation is misleading. James Madison, at the time of the foundation of democracy in America, praised civil society as a guarantee of liberty because by being 'broken into so many parts, interests and classes of citizens', it curbs even majority rule. No word describes better the 'parts, interests and classes of citizens' which civil society is about than *association*. The creative chaos of associations coalesces as if guided by an invisible hand into the setting in which the greatest number find the greatest life chances. In economic terms, the market describes that setting; in political terms, it is the public. Nowadays, both are mediated in numerous ways; the days of simple markets, or indeed of the public assembling outside the town hall for debate and decision, are almost gone. But the principles of both are still valid. The market and the public are where the associations of civil society interact.

In other words, there is such a thing as society. What is more, there has to be if we do not want to end up in a state of anomy. The word, association, also indicates the necessary element of cohesion in civil society. Dan Horowitz put it well: 'Social cohesion does not necessarily imply social homogeneity or harmony or absence of social tensions.' It does, by contrast, have certain positive implications. Apart from the indispensable framework of the rule of law, the associations of civil society represent values of trust and cooperation, and of inclusion. A civil society is a society of citizens who have rights and accept obligations, and who behave in a civil and civilized manner towards each other. It is a society which tries to make sure that no one is excluded, and which offers its members a sense of belonging as well as a constitution of liberty.

This is no Utopia. For a century after the Civil War the United States of America was certainly driven by the aspiration to be such a civil society. The same can be said for the United Kingdom during the larger part of the twentieth century. In Canada and Australia, but also in Sweden and Switzerland, other versions of achieving the same aspirations could be found. For a while after the Second World War, the entire First World was in these terms quite a good place to live. The trouble is that so many of these statements now have to be made in the past tense. Somehow or other, either prosperity or civility or liberty (if not two of these or even all three) have taken a knock almost everywhere. That is why rebuilding civil society under new conditions is so important.

What then of the fourth city in my tale? First of all, it has to be a city. Whether it numbers 40 000, 180 000 or 2.5 million inhabitants, it must be an identifiable community with a strong sense of local commitment and institutions to match it. The city itself is an element of civil society. In economic terms, a variety of companies of different sizes and branches of business is obviously desirable. More important, indeed essential for economic well-being is, however, a combination of competitiveness and stakeholder involvement. If one wants to avoid fashionable language one could say that companies need to seek arrangements which assure as far as possible their long-term success and engender relations of trust and commitment with all who are involved in their fortunes. This is actually what many companies are groping for today, and the best provide benchmarks for the rest. Individuals have to respond to the analogous dual challenge of flexibility and security. People's lives will look different than they did in the days of old-style careers in an expectation of full employment. Security is no longer built into the world of work, or of education for that matter; people have to carry it with and within them, which means that their entitlements have to be transportable, and their strength lies in the skills, including the ability to go on adjusting and enhancing them. There are signs that women find it easier to cope with the new balance of flexibility and security than men; perhaps they had to do so earlier. In institutional as well as personal terms, associations in the narrow and the organized sense will play a major part. The tradition of voluntarism, of volunteering as well as charitable giving, will see a new flowering. The result will be untidy and imperfect, it will not do away with pain and fear, or with conflict but it may point the way to a prosperous, civil and liberal world.

My first city was in North America, the second in Continental Europe, the third in South East Asia – it would be fitting if the fourth emerged in the country to which this thank-offering is given, Britain.

Understanding Change

8   The Democratic Revolution, or the Uses of the Science of Politics

Address on the occasion of the conferment of an Honorary Doctorate of Political Science by the University of Bologna, delivered at Forli on 30 May 1991

First of all, I want to thank the University of Bologna and its Faculty of Political Sciences for the signal honour which they have bestowed upon me. This honorary degree makes me feel not just grateful but humble. I take special pleasure in the fact that it is given at a time at which the Faculty of Political Sciences is branching out into new directions both intellectually and geographically. The establishment of the section on international relations here in Forli shows that the University is seeking new ways forward; it is reforming.

I like reform. Once or twice in my life, I have been involved in the creation of entirely new institutions, including a university. I can understand the excitement which goes with such ventures, but myself find more satisfaction in the transformation of old structures. Institutions are both wonderful achievements of the civilized mind and challenges to the reforming spirit. They need to be preserved and reformed at the same time. I am anything but a Hegelian, and rarely quote the father of the dreadful twins of modern illiberalism – fascism and communism – with approval, but here I am reminded of the triple meaning of the German word, *aufheben*, which Hegel liked to use to describe the dialectical process: it is necessary to overcome institutions, to preserve them, and to lift them to a higher level. Like John Maynard Keynes's, my radical liberalism of thought and politics is tempered by the conservative inclination to defend life within existing institutions. Thus I am happy on this occasion on which the Faculty of Political Sciences of this ancient university is engaged in a new venture.

The name of the Faculty also gives pause for thought: *political sciences*. What a wonderful hope! At least, I think it is wonderful. In Britain we had until recently a prime minister who actually banned the word, social science, and forced the Social Science Research Council to rename itself. (It is now called Economic and Social Research Council.) The science of society was forbidden by decree. What a change from the optimism of David Hume, who

83

wrote in his *Treatise* 250 years ago that his 'attempt to introduce the experimental method of reasoning into moral subjects' would soon lead to the emergence of a 'science of man' which 'will not be inferior in certainty, and will be much superior in utility to any other human comprehension'. Margaret Thatcher is of course not the only one who has observed that this has in fact not happened. Her own view may be related to her belief (expressed in an interview with a women's magazine) that 'there is no such thing as society'. If society does not exist there clearly cannot be a science which tries to make sense of it. Even those who do not go quite so far, however, would claim that 'society', or whatever this shorthand expression stands for, cannot be studied in quite the same way as 'nature'. We shall never know what goes on in the human mind (they say), and the best we can offer in our endeavours to come to grips with social and political events is to apply the historian's talents to them, *Verstehen* (as Max Weber and his contemporaries called it), an informed empathy which brings to light the multiple dimensions of events and thereby gives them meaning.

This is no mean achievement if indeed it is achieved. To be sure, some modern historians would like to go rather further. The *Annales* school would not accept the traditional notion of history. In their wake, many historians have come to apply the methods of social science to their data. Yet clearly a deep understanding of particular events and individual actions is both difficult and useful. But it is not science. Poets and writers may tell us how and even why a particular apple falls from a particular tree at a particular time, or how and why an individual catches a cold in Forli today; but natural scientists are not even trying to explain such unique events. They are concerned with underlying structures, with gravity, with viruses. This is probably what Hume and others had in mind when they tried to initiate a social and political science in Scotland around the time of the industrial revolution. Why have we made so little progress along this road? What makes it still possible, 250 years later, to doubt that there can ever be a science of man?

The reason is, I believe, that we have not tried hard enough. We have simply not had the courage of our convictions. I can hear the challenge: speak for yourself! (Which is exactly what I shall do in a moment.) Is there not economics, both as economic theory and as econometrics? Are there not the experimental branches of psychology, including social psychology? Indeed, do we not have important theories of a sociological or politological character? But also, is not the very intention to emulate science with respect to society barren?

It is time to turn to examples, big examples, for my dream has long been the scientific study of total societies. For most of us, the revolution of 1989 is one of the great events of our lifetime. Even now that it has gone somewhat sour, it reminds us of the horizons of the open society, and of the force of freedom under the most unlikely conditions. I was about to say: even now that it has *predictably* gone somewhat sour ... You would have accepted that statement perhaps, without realizing that it implies a whole theory. But let me first look at another aspect of our knowledge of revolutions. Why did we not predict that 1989 would happen? Why did it come as such a surprise? The other day, I stumbled across the minutes of a committee meeting held in October 1989. There, great pleasure was expressed at the events in Poland and East Germany; it was said that Czechoslovakia would probably follow suit one day, though this might take some time; but, it was added, Bulgaria, Romania, let alone Albania were unfortunately destined to remain dictatorships for some time to come. Thus in October 1989! Why do we not have a social science which could have warned us at least at that late hour that our assumptions were wrong?

This is where I must, for a moment, speak for myself. One of my former students (the German theorist of international relations, Dieter Senghaas) recently pointed out to me that in my early essays on social conflict, I had predicted exactly what would happen in countries with a 'monistic' (today I would say, monopolistic) structure. In 1957, I stated quite unambiguously that structures designed to suppress conflict could and would not last, but would explode and lead to rapid and radical changes, and that the only question was when the political conditions of organizations are such that the underlying social forces can find expression. At the time, I referred explicitly to the Communist countries of Eastern Europe. However, when I wrote *The Modern Social Conflict* thirty years later, I had become much more cautious. Now I argued that there are many ways in which conflicts can find expression. Even the monopolistic party can serve as a safety valve for criticism as well as an instrument of control. *Détente* may help to let off steam. It was, therefore, (I said in 1988) quite difficult to tell when or even whether really existing socialism would cease to be viable.

In other words, the courage of my convictions had become smothered in experience. I was now submerged in the contingencies which have to do with when the particular apple falls, and lost sight of the law of gravity. Perhaps one has to be young to think of structures in all their purity. (After all, even scientists tend to get the Nobel Prize for work which they did rather early in their careers.) Certainly, at 28 I was quite sure of my theories, if not of myself. Now, the latter may no longer be an issue, but theoretical certainties have been dissipated in the process.

This is a pity. Let me make a few statements which are relevant to the revolution of 1989 and its consequences; they are put in fairly simple language but are meant to be theoretical statements about political structures:

- Monopolistic classes may suppress opposition but this merely turns manifest conflicts into latent conflicts.
- The more rigidly monopolistic classes enforce their rule, the more absolute will opposition demands become.
- Latent conflict becomes manifest once certain basic political conditions of organization are given.
- In a monopolistic structure a spark of hope for change will set the powder keg of revolution on fire.
- (In such a situation, *glasnost* and *perestroika* are incompatible: freedom of speech and association means revolution, and restructuring can only be achieved with a high degree of control.)
- Revolutionary change leads to the replacement of ruling groups but also to the dismantling of the machinery of government.
- The revolutionary process involves the collapse of the centre, thus a tendency towards anarchy and anomy.
- Anarchy and anomy lead to calls for the (re-)establishment of effective power, even by groups or individuals which make (old or new) monopolistic claims.
- There is no straight and painless road from monopolistic structures of power to pluralism and democracy.

Let me stop here. If the statements which I have made are true, they provide a powerful instrument of analysis. They are abstract statements, of course, which need to be filled in. I have done this in one case by mentioning *glasnost* and *perestroika*. Clearly, President Gorbachev comes into the picture somewhere, and perhaps the Helsinki process and other events. Even so, the statements encourage me to tell you of another dream which I have long cherished in relation to the science of society. Every night, when after the television news the weatherman appears on the screen, I have a vision. Here is the learned meteorologist pointing to a map of Europe and sometimes the world, and telling us about westerly winds bringing yet another area of low pressure across the Atlantic with rain to follow, though in the south high pressure and warm temperatures continue. Why (I say to myself) is this man not followed, or even preceded, by a sociopolitical weatherman? A deep economic and political depression with its centre in Moscow remains stable; where it meets areas of higher pressure over the Baltic states and the Ukraine, violent thunderstorms are likely; most of Western Europe remains variable but fine, with isolated showers in a number of places, though the fog over the Brussels area refuses to lift and the jetstream from the United States brings threatening clouds in both trade and defence matters ... Frivolous? Perhaps a little. Yet I think that we could, and perhaps do, know as much about important social trends as meteorologists do about the climate and the weather. Indeed, in both cases the basic truth is simple. I am told that the safest weather prediction is always that tomorrow will be like today. This is true in at least 80 per cent of all cases. Change, major change at that, is the exception rather than the rule.

This makes it all the more interesting. Returning to the serious statements which I offered about monopolistic rule, revolution and democracy, the question is: how useful are these statements? How much do they tell us about real events? At first sight, not very much at all. It is hard to point to a single case which conforms to the structure of change implied by my statements. Poland and Hungary were examples of what Timothy Garton Ash called *refolutions* rather than revolutions. Reforms from above corresponded to, and absorbed pressure from, below. In one case, a Round Table assembled government and opposition and thus dismantled the monopoly. In the other case, economic activity was used as a safety valve for political opposition. Then there is the strange case of East Germany, where the revolution was terminated by conquest, as it were, by the West German takeover. Other specific observations come to mind. In Bulgaria, Romania and most recently Albania, elections were held at a time at which what I called the political conditions of organization were as yet quite incomplete. As a result, new democratic forces had a chance in the cities but were beaten in the countryside so that it could appear as if the people had given legitimacy to remnants of the old regime.

Such specific observations are highly relevant for the normative question which many would wish to ask: will democracy work in the countries which have shed communism? The proper answer to this question is not abstract and structural, but specific and even cultural. Democracy, like the market economy, has many forms. No two countries practice it in the same manner. Even similar constitutional arrangements can provide a framework for very different constitutional realities. Italy and Britain are both parliamentary democracies, but their political cultures could hardly be more different. A similar statement can be made about the presidential democracies of France and the United States. Thus, every one of the new democracies of Europe is likely to find its own pattern, and some of these patterns may defy the predictions of failure which can be derived from the theory of revolutionary change.

Yet we should not too readily or easily abandon the claims of a general and theoretical social science. Even within the realm of political change, every one of the new democracies will have to answer a number of questions. For example: how can the new political class command a machinery of government which makes the exercise of power effective without handing it back to the *nomenklatura*? And in the same vein: how can the rule of law be established when there is no untainted judiciary and no understanding of the independence of the third power? Even technical questions of political structures are not easily answered: how will political parties sort themselves out once the anti-monopolistic alliance breaks up? And of course: how are countries going to find a balance between the twin needs of popular legitimation and stable government? These are, moreover, questions which arise even before we get to the deeper issues of the economic valley of tears and its political consequences, and of the absence of a civil society to sustain political institutions. The questions are informed by theories. Without doubt they look different in different contexts, and thus can be answered differently; but they have to be answered. Theoretical analysis guides us to the critical issues of practical action.

What if the questions are not answered satisfactorily? This takes us back to my earlier comment that the revolution of 1989 has 'predictably' gone somewhat sour. What can we say about the consequences of this predictable process? Not much that gives cause for optimism. The consequences of the inability on the part of the new political class to become a plausible governing class are dire. Governments will promise and even legislate, but nothing much will happen on the ground. With the ineffectiveness of legislation, law and order begin to be put at risk. The centre does not hold; thus the parts begin to drift off, and often turn against each other. People look for bonds which take the place of the social contract in its dual meaning as a contract of association and a contract of government. Even these bonds do not automatically create viable units. The phantasies of Jean-Jacques Rousseau and Jürgen Habermas overlook the Hobbesian problem of order and the likelihood that it will be resolved by Hobbesian answers. Self-appointed leaders will emerge who play on people's fears and establish themselves in the name of self-determination, national independence, or simply law and order.

All this seems plausible to us because we can see it before our own eyes. The Soviet Union may provide the clearest illustration of the failure of transformation; but we have not seen the end of the process in any of the other formerly communist countries, not even in the five new *Länder* of Germany. Clearly the transition from monopolistic rule to democracy is more difficult than that from democracy to totalitarianism. Totalitarian rulers can use the existing machinery of government and pervert it; democratic rulers have to start from scratch, and worse, from a state of profound demoralization.

The probability of failure is high. It is, therefore, critical for the rest of us who have been fortunate to live in freedom for the last 45 years to do everything we can in order to reduce this probability. This means the inclusion of the new democracies in Europe in every sense of the word. The detail is a subject for another time and another place.

You will have noticed that I have attempted to roll two lectures into one short address. On the one hand I have tried to cast a little light on a subject of passionate interest which is also the subject of my recent *Reflections on the Revolution in Europe*. On the other hand I have offered some ideas on the nature and place of a social science which is worthy of this name. This is – or should I say: would be? – a set of theories which have to do with the underlying structures of observed events. Such theories do not describe real events. Worse still (at least for the methodological purist), real events are invariably complicated by specific conditions of culture and history to such an extent that it is almost impossible to set up circumstances which could be said to falsify theories. *Almost* impossible – there may yet be a way to get round this difficulty. Even so, theories of society, including sociopolitical and socio-economic theories, are an indispensable backbone to any sustained understanding of social processes. They lead us to important questions and help us identify what is peculiar and unique in given processes, if nothing else. They take us beyond the poetic arbitrariness of mere *Verstehen*, although the poetry of great historiography may get lost in the process.

Theory is never a purpose in itself, although it can be beautiful and thus satisfy the aesthetic sense of scholars. In the natural sciences, theory is useful for purposes of application, if only to the nightly weather forecast after the television news. In the social sciences, theory helps produce what I like to call social analysis. This is the theoretically informed attempt to make sense of real processes. My *Reflections* are undoubtedly imperfect, but they are an attempt of this kind. One can think of other important examples of social analysis. One of my favourites is T.H. Marshall's little book on *Citizenship and Social Class*. (Most examples of social analysis are 'little books'.) Twenty years earlier, Theodor Geiger produced his compelling analysis of 'The Middle Classes and National Socialism' in his book on German social stratification. Max Weber's *Protestant Ethic and the Spirit of Capitalism* belongs in the same category, and so does Karl Marx's *18th Brumaire of Louis Bonaparte*. Let us not despair therefore of the chances of a science of man as David Hume saw it. This Faculty of Political Sciences can lead the way and thus add further distinction to a great university.

9   Who Makes History? On the Entanglements of Economics and Politics

Opening Address to the International Economic History Congress, delivered at the Teatro della Scala, Milan, on 12 September 1994

It is an unusual pleasure for me to address this Congress, though your opening speaker cannot claim to be an economic historian. I have praised your discipline but never practised it. Such praise was easy to justify in looking at the London School of Economics whose centenary history I have recently written. The founding Director, W.A.S. Hewins, was an economic historian – or was he more a late nineteenth-century historical economist? As the social sciences unfolded, such ambiguities gave way to tidier departmental divisions. While Lionel Robbins and Friedrich von Hayek on the one hand, and Harold Laski on the other, took economics and politics down their increasingly separate paths, Arthur Bowley and Roy Allen advanced, under the name of statistics, sample research and econometrics and other quantitative sports, and the Director, Sir William (later Lord) Beveridge, sought to promote social biology as the only truly scientific branch of social studies. Yet students in the interwar years flocked to R.H. Tawney and his colleagues, Michael Postan, Eileen Power. Perhaps the economic historians were simply nicer than the rest, but there was – and is – something special about the discipline too. The anthropologist Bronislaw Malinowski meant it as a compliment of course when he described economic history as the social anthropology of the past. Today, economic history is the only social science left which combines as a matter of course the descriptive and the theoretical, the qualitative and the quantitative, indeed economics and history and much in between.

By contrast, your opening speaker is a social scientist of no particular description, and one who has strayed into practical domains at that. It may therefore be pardonable if I begin my remarks with a topical reference. One of the breathtaking events of recent months is the incipient emergence of peace in the Middle East. Suddenly the mood of the region is changing. One of the architects, and at the same time interpreters, of the process is Israel's visionary foreign minister Shimon Peres. 'In the past we had enemies' I heard him say with one of his catching phrases, 'now we have problems'. Enemies set people against each other in confrontation and war; problems force people to get together and to cooperate. The change is not just one of style but also one of substance. Enemies live in a world of politics; but the problems are economic. In his book on *The New Middle East*, Peres is quite explicit. Here are some of his words:

> Fate has brought us from a world of territorial conflict to one of economic challenge and of new opportunities created by human intellectual advances.

Or again:

> As long as the Middle East's food supply is inadequate, and new food sources grow at a slower rate than does the region's population, distress will continue – as will its political expression, whether in the form of the black hoods of revolutionaries or the white robes of religious fanatics.

And then, with an almost philosophical sweep:

> Until the end of the twentieth century, the general concept of history was rooted in the European model of national politics, springing from the world of nationalist values and symbols. The next era will be increasingly based on the Asiatic model of national politics, drawn from the world of economic values, whose fundamental principle is exploitation of knowledge to maximize profit.

Does anyone remember that this is a socialist, at any rate a social democrat speaking? The question to which I want to address myself in these remarks could not be put more succinctly: after politics, economics? Are we entering an era in which economic motives dominate political action? Will economic advances resolve the problems which traditional politics failed to cope with? Are we witnessing the abdication of professional politicians in favour of businessmen and professors of economics? And perhaps the abdication of Europe and civil liberties and democracy in favour of Asia and efficiency and authoritarianism?

Other hopeful recent events and their protagonists could have been cited to set out the issues. President Mandela is convinced that if, and only if, the economic promises of the new South Africa can be kept and the many be freed from misery, national unity and political democracy will be sustainable. Simon Peres's expectation that economic growth will put paid to terrorism and fundamentalism has been expressed elsewhere as well, in Northern Ireland for example, where many have argued: 'Give them jobs and they will drop their guns!' Nor are such views confined to dramatic changes. The Italian foreign minister Martino was heard saying: 'Trade unites, politics divides.' The 1980s were certainly a period in the OECD world in which many believed that politicians had made a mess of things, and it was now time to let businessmen, or perhaps more abstract forces, business, the economy, have a go. Those who did not believe this, such as Chancellor Kohl of Germany, are now accused of having wreaked havoc economically by imposing purely political decisions on post-communist East Germany. A new *economism* has come to dominate public discourse which makes one wonder whether Marxism, which seemed well and truly dead, is celebrating an unexpected revival in capitalist circles where the prevailing creed seems to be: trust economic forces, and politics will come right by itself! Politics is the 'fatal conceit', economics the real basis of any progress. But then, it would be more than a little unfair to call Hayek an implicit Marxist.

Speaking of Hayek, one further set of observations must be introduced before we can begin to try and sort matters out. In East Central Europe, four years of often disappointing experiences have added to the sophistication of those who believe in the primacy of economic reform. When the Oxford political theorist John Gray attacked the Harvard economist Jeffrey Sachs for his 'big bang' approach to economic reform, Sachs replied that he had always believed in both the importance of institutions and the cultural diversity of economic structures. In looking back to his own heroic and crucially important reforms during Poland's first post-communist government, Leszek Balcerowicz described 'post-communist transitions' as but one of several kinds of transition, including the 'classical transition' of nineteenth-century countries, the 'new classical transition' of, for example, West Germany after 1945, 'market oriented reforms in non-communist countries' like Argentina or Chile, and, slightly mysteriously as may be appropriate, the 'Asian post communist transition'. On the scope of the post-communist experience Balcerowicz says: 'Both political and economic systems are affected, and changes in these systems in turn interact with changes in the social structure.' Similarly, the most enthusiastic reformer of the present, the Czech Prime Minister Vaclav Klaus, speaks of the 'specific interplay of political and economic factors in the transformation process'. But in the end he comes down to a Hayekian belief in economic forces putting everything right once they are given half a chance:

> Monetarism, not Keynesianism; fixed rules, not fine-tuning; balanced budget, not fiscal activism; self-reliance, not dependence on foreign mercenaries; these are the inspiring words for all of us who want to accomplish the historic transformation, for all of us who want to create a free, democratic and efficient society.

Who then makes history? Is it statesmen or impersonal economic forces? Is it compelling political constraints or entrepreneurs? There may be a case for not getting too involved in the debate about leadership and circumstances in the present context. Great analysts of the circumstances of modern societies, like Joseph Schumpeter or Max Weber, have ended up extolling the virtues of creative destruction by entrepreneurs, or of leaders who break the bars of the iron cage of bureaucratic bondage. The interplay of individual initiative and social conditions might well be the subject of another congress (and probably one of political science). Here, the central question is: how do the values, interests, structures of the economy on the one hand, and the polity on the other, interact? Which of them dominate when? Which of them should have primacy? How are they at all times, and notably in our age, entangled? What, if anything, do we do about their entanglements?

Theory is not a proper subject for an opening address. In any case I am too old for this pastime of twenty- and perhaps thirty-somethings. Let me state therefore without much claim to theoretical subtlety that in my understanding there is a significant difference between the political and the economic approach. Democracy is a political concept, market processes are economic. Some notions sit uneasily on the border. You will note that I spoke of market processes; the rules of a market economy are politico–economic. So are currencies. It is hard to decide whether monetary union is an economic or a political concept. As I use the term, politics is about rules, entitlements, whereas economics is about provisions, gradations of supply and demand. Political issues are in principle about saying yes or no, even if compromise is the civilized method of dealing with many of them (though not, for example, with human rights). Economic issues are in principle about more or less, 2.8 per cent growth rather than −1.1 per cent. Economic inequalities become a political issue only if they sustain privilege or exclusion, which means in effect that they turn into entitlements or the lack of them, which can no longer be overcome by gradual, quantitative improvements or reductions.

Great economists have always tried to integrate entitlements and provisions in their theories. John Maynard Keynes probably succeeded, and he claimed that Alfred Marshall before him had done so. In our time, Amartya Sen linked famines to entitlements, and also to specific rights like freedom of the press. Where free expression prevails, mass deprivation becomes a public scandal which is not tolerable. Partha Dasgupta, in speaking of 'destitution and well-being', includes human rights in his concept of 'social well-being'. Thus there may be such an endeavour as 'political economy'. But it remains a troubled union. Economists are as tempted to dissolve entitlement questions into issues of more or less, as political scientists are to translate economic issues into structures of partisan conflict. An economic theory of democracy makes sense only where all major constitutional questions have been resolved, and society is a level playing-field.

But enough of such hints. They are relevant for these reflections but they also detract from real issues. Two of them will be the subject of my remaining time. The first takes us back to transitions or transformations. They tell us a great deal about the entanglements of economics and politics, and at least some of the lessons must be mentioned. The second real issue is even more serious. It has to do with Shimon Peres's philosophy of history, that is with the ascendancy of Asian values. Both, I believe, are as relevant to the OECD world as they are to the rest.

The lessons of major transformations, and notably of the post-communist transition, for our understanding of economic and politics are many. If I single out five, there is no magic about the number. The first lesson has to do with what happens before transitions begin, with the instability of the old regime. Its apparently inevitable collapse and the compelling need for a new beginning – whether we call it revolution or not – always involves an element of economic mismanagement on the part of the rulers and resentment on the part of the ruled. Crane Brinton, in his *Anatomy of Revolution*, saw this as related to public expenditure. An evident mismatch of taxes and services, of claims on the incomes of citizens and provisions for their benefit, politicizes, as it were, the economic condition. If those in power are seen to do well whereas the condition of the majority deteriorates, the status quo can become unsustainable, and a revolutionary situation builds up. If people can watch on television or otherwise find out how others not far from them fare – as happened in the Communist countries during the OECD boom of the 1980s – the spark of hope for the better is thrown into the revolutionary powder keg. In any case, economic frustration can have political consequences all the way to regime changes.

Secondly, the first step of regime changes is clearly political. A new set of values – of hegemonial values perhaps – and possibly a whole new political class is needed to set in motion institutional reforms and create the framework of rules and agencies needed for economic development. One may be tempted to state more generally that at critical points of history it is political action rather than economic forces that matter. Even inveterate Hayekians have to bring about fixed rules, a balanced budget, privatization laws and a stable currency by political action. Balcerowicz speaks in this context of 'extraordinary politics', politics above and beyond the ordinary demands on action, and distinguishes it from 'normal politics' which is the desired result though one which is not quickly attainable.

Thirdly, the path to prospering (market) economies leads through a valley of tears. For the majority, economic conditions get worse before they get better. One must hope that Minister Peres's and King Hussein's and many others' vision for a new Middle East will come true. However, bitter experiences tell us that the route from a per capita income of 1200 dollars to one of 24 000 dollars begins with a phase of social disruption and general disorientation. In this phase, people are if anything more susceptible to fundamentalist (or nationalist, or otherwise 'integrist') temptations. Poland is possibly the only post-communist country which has passed through the bottom of the valley (though the Czech government would claim the same if not more for its country too). Even President Mandela may find that as he begins his promised redistribution, the economic cake which he inherited from the old regime is at least initially shrinking, and South Africa will enter a period of extreme precariousness for both the economy and the polity.

Fourthly, the successful trek through the valley of tears and the stabilization of economic reforms more generally raise another set of political questions. They are questions of 'constraint' (to use Paul Collier's notion for developing economies). There have to be ways – institutions, powers – to prevent things from getting out of hand – by governments giving in to popular demands and sacrificing budget stability and soon the currency in the process; by a loss of political credibility which destroys credit-worthiness; by a decline in political stability which deters investment and trade. This was, and is, one of the great Latin American dilemmas. Mexico seems to have coped with it, by the combination of an election opened to the scrutiny of international observers, and NAFTA; Argentina has unfortunately added an institutional gamble to its economic success story; Brazil seems to find it hard to get out of its politico–economic turmoil.

Constraint can be made effective in two ways (and they are often related). One is the stubborn defence of domestic institutions – of the constitution – against all challenges and temptations. This requires almost superhuman leadership qualities, and is helped by personal charisma. The other is external support. Beyond funding infrastructure projects, the postwar Marshall Plan provided above all that external constraint, including an organization to impose it, OEEC, the predecessor of today's OECD. Spain and Portugal sought, and to some extent found, an equivalent in the European Community. Some African countries still benefit from the French Franc Zone, however much they may mind the dependence which it involves. So far as Eastern Europe is concerned, European institutions have so far failed to do what is needed. In South Africa, as in so many other parts of the world, the residual hegemonial power of the United States of America is still the only source of benevolent constraint.

The fifth point is more in the nature of a sigh than an analytical statement: lucky the country which has managed to set both market economy and political democracy on course and then separated the two sufficiently in fact and in people's minds to leave the economy to its own resources and keep democracy stable, even at times of recession and economic crisis. In the interwar period there were few to which this lucky condition applied: the United States, Britain, parts of the British Commonwealth, smaller countries like Sweden and Switzerland. They came through the great Depression fundamentally unchallenged if not unscathed and were never really afflicted by the temptations of totalitarianism. Almost fifty years after the Second World War, one must hope that others have joined this core group of free and prosperous countries. Germany is one of them, though the generic problem of Weimar Germany has not gone away: when the economic going gets rough, people begin to doubt the constitution of liberty and embrace illiberal political projects.

In an abstract sense this may seem strange. After all, market economies and political democracies have their basic principle in common. They are both viable – some would say, the only viable – responses to the human condition of uncertainty in which arrangements are needed to make change without disruption and violence possible. Market economies accommodate changes both in taste and in technology, thus on the demand as well as the supply side. Democracies accommodate changes in people's interests and preferences. However, the symmetry of the two does not imply, or necessarily result in, their joint development. Political democracy does not follow from the presence of an effective market economy, nor is such an economy the automatic result of democratic political conditions. Worse than that – and this is the second major issue on which I promised a few comments – modern economic development seems to favour authoritarian rather than democratic government.

Authoritarian does not mean totalitarian. Authoritarian regimes are not based on permanent mobilization nor do they require a Great Leader and a pervasive ideology. But they do involve a closed public class which is unwilling to relinquish power and therefore self-perpetuating. They are the guardians of values which are defined as duties for everyone; violations are firmly and visibly stamped on. Anyone who complies and contributes to economic advance is left alone, though not to watch pornographic videos, read the *Far Eastern Economic Review* or discuss Marx's theories of the relationship between economics and politics. For the passing visitor, authoritarian countries are often attractive and comforting; for the native they are demanding but also predictable; for the poet, the inventor, the financial-market whiz kid with extravagant tastes, to say nothing of the investigative reporter, the eccentric and the liberal, they are unbearable.

The flippant allusions are not meant to minimize a major problem, indeed a series of major problems which are all related to the central theme of these remarks. The series begins with the initial phase of economic development. Economic historians have – ever since R.H. Tawney – qualified Max Weber's thesis about protestantism and the rise of capitalism in numerous ways. However, the underlying problem remains. In order to take off, capitalism (to use the somewhat misleading shorthand) requires a readiness on the part of many to forego the pleasure of immediately enjoying the fruits of economic success. A time of deferred gratification – more technically, of savings and investment – is needed before consumption and enjoyment. It may well be that at some point in history, and in some cultures, such deferred gratification corresponded to an individual morality backed by Calvinist or Lutheran beliefs. By the nineteenth century, however, economic development could no longer be founded on the expectation of puritanical self-denial alone. 'Imperial Germany and the Industrial Revolution' (as Thorstein Veblen pointed out before the First World War) was a story of savings and investments encouraged, and if need be enforced, by an authoritarian state. Many others have followed suit, and those who did not – like the great democracy, India – may have lagged in economic development for that reason among others. In any case, at a time at which Western capitalism is motivated not so much by people's propensity to save, nor even by the hedonist pleasures of immediate consumption, but by borrowing and thus by anticipated gratification, it is hard to persuade anyone anywhere without a degree of compulsion to save and wait.

The next problem arises during transitions. It is in part political. If we are to believe Brinton – and there are good reasons to do so – the 'rule of the moderates' which follows regime changes cannot last. The instruments of government are crumbling in the tender hands of dissidents-turned-rulers, and their benevolence is ill-suited to the tough task of rebuilding them. The economic predicament does not help. The trek through the valley of tears calls for firm and to some extent insensitive leadership. This does not go very well with the spirit of the new democratic institutions. Poland responded to this predicament by sacking the reformer, Balcerowicz, while keeping his reforms in place. Others have retreated and left the scene to an unsavoury combination of speculators, mafiosi, even gangsters, and old *nomenklatura* faces. The Czech Prime Minister pursues what for the time being can still be called a democratic authoritarianism which has borrowed from Western examples, notably from Margaret Thatcher, a curious stance. It clearly defines friend and foe, opposes civil society as the resource of the foes, and strengthens central government and its many unaccountable agencies for the benefit of the friends. As long as the people are free to elect an alternative government such authoritarianism remains in one sense democratic; still, while it may help create economically efficient societies they are hardly models of liberty.

However, the most serious authoritarian threat lurks precisely where so many seek salvation, in 'the Asiatic model of national politics, drawn from the world of economic values'. In the Western world, several trends have conspired to dent and even destroy social cohesion. Some would say that it all started with the 1960s and the 'permissive society'. Others point the finger at the 'casino capitalism' of the 1980s with its 'get rich quick' approach which set people against each other and left many behind. Long-term unemployment especially of the young, is growing in most countries, and where it is not, a new poverty is spreading fast. The syndrome of inner-city blight, family and community disintegration, drugs and crime is no longer confined to ghettos; it affects everybody. At the same time, the globalization of markets and the ensuing competition makes massive, often painful demands on companies, communities and individuals. At times, the requirements of wealth creation seem to aggravate problems of social cohesion. In any case, people are confused; a sense of anomy is spreading, and with it the latent, and at times the manifest, search for authority.

This is where to some what I shall call Asian authoritarianism begins to look like an attractive alternative. A number of the new rich countries of the world, notably in Asia, appear to have watched the West and decided that they were going to have growth without the side-effects. They proceeded to restrict democratic liberties and back up their insistence on more traditional values by strong public authorities in the hands of a self-perpetuating political class. They also began to lecture Europeans, and even more incessantly, Americans, on their inability to maintain cohesive societies, that is on rotting cities, single mothers, young drug addicts and crime, crime, crime. The lectures fell – and fall – on fertile ground. Worrying ambiguities creep into statements by leading Western figures, as in a recent interview with the media mogul Rupert Murdoch:

> Singapore is not liberal but clean and free of drug addicts. Not so long ago it was an impoverished, exploited colony with famine, diseases and other problems. Now people find themselves in three-room apartments, with jobs and clean streets. Countries like Singapore are going the right way: material incentives create business and the free market economy as well as perhaps a middle class and with it democracy. If politicians try it the other way round with immediate democracy, the Russian model is the result. 90 per cent of the Chinese are more interested in a better material life than in the right to vote.

Thus the world of economic values becomes one that may be efficient but is hardly free and democratic.

It is time to take stock. There is, to put it mildly, no guarantee that a politics informed by economic interest sustains democratic institutions and free societies. At every stage of economic development the risk of authoritarianism is as great if not greater than the prospect of democracy. What does this tell us about the relations between economics and politics? Is the primacy of politics as much a desirable objective as a historical fact? Politics to the politicians, as it were? Or are there more subtle relations between entitlements and provisions, liberty and efficiency, politics and economics?

The latter is certainly the case. My three brief conclusions are not intended to summarize the arguments, affirmations and allusions of this lecture. They are at best pointers for further thought and perhaps an expression of my own value preferences.

First, it would appear that the turning points of history are the results of political processes and decisions rather than economic forces. The British politician who stated categorically that in his view there is no economic power, but power is always political, may have gone rather far. But constitutional, and more generally 'extra-ordinary' politics can, and does override economic interest and even economic advantage.

Secondly, the greatest life chances of the greatest number are probably best realized in periods of 'normal' politics, that is to say, when politics does not matter all that much for people. They can get on with things without having to look over their shoulders to authorities. The economy can prosper and civil society can flourish. Well-being extends far beyond the material domain. This is not an Arcadia, let alone a Utopia, for in some countries of today's OECD world such conditions existed for considerable periods of time. Even in these countries, however, there is no guarantee that they will last.

Finally, when economic values begin to dominate politics, liberty is often at risk. The new economism of capitalists is no less illiberal than the old one of Marxists. It may not raise the spectre of totalitarianism but its authoritarian potential is a source of concern.

Who then should make history? There is not much evidence that professional politicians are particularly good at running businesses, though many have retired to boardrooms and the often handsome material rewards of state-sponsored banks and other enterprises. On the other hand, businessmen or even professors of economics are not necessarily better at steering the ship of state. In one sense, professional specialisms do not matter; what matters, is the personality of leaders. Yet if Max Weber had added a third lecture to the two on 'Science as a Vocation' and 'Politics as a Vocation', entitled 'Business as a Vocation' he might well have identified important differences. Politics is always a balancing act between ideas, support, and institutions. At least in democracies, politicians have to know where they want to go, marshal the necessary support for it among voters and social groups, and move forward within a highly structured environment of rules and institutions. Businessmen tend to find this cumbersome, and professors of economics regard it as wasteful. They are as a result first impatient and then inclined to more authoritarian ways. They are often lacking that sense of history which is the hallmark of great political leaders. Perhaps we need a mixture of both, of the economists' sense of efficiency and the historians' sense of institutions. Dare I say it? Perhaps economic historians have the answer.

10   Whither Social Sciences?

Sixth Annual Lecture of the Economic and Social Research Council (ESRC), given on 19 October 1995, at the Royal Society of Arts in London

Much printers' ink has flowed, and ebbed, in the 250 years since David Hume staked the claim for a social science to equal the natural sciences. His *Treatise of Human Nature* bore the subtitle 'An attempt to introduce the experimental method of reasoning into moral subjects'. In the Introduction of 1739 he explained that an interval of one hundred years between the birth of experimental natural and social sciences was quite normal because a century had similarly separated the Greek origins of the two branches of knowledge. (He had in mind Thales as the first natural scientist and Socrates as the first social scientist.) Now, however, in the early eighteenth century, people 'have begun to put the science of man on a new footing ... Nor ought we to think that this latter improvement in the science of man will do less honour to our native country than the former in natural philosophy but ought rather to esteem it a greater glory, upon account of the greater importance of that science , as well as the necessity it lay under of such a reformation.'

Adam Smith notwithstanding – and Smith not only believed in social science but saw political economy 'as a branch of the science of a statesman or legislator' – the governments of the country to which the social sciences had been intended to do such honour were in the end so unimpressed that they caused the Social Science Research Council to change its name. Research? Perhaps. Science? No. Britain is, of course, my country now though in my native country, language might have helped prevent such fundamentalism: *Wissenschaft – Sozialwissenschaft –* is a much more generous concept than 'science' and 'social science'. But fundamentalism it remains if governments take it upon themselves to meddle even in matters of epistemology. Dare I say it? – *Eppur si muove.* Not the globe in this case, but social science moves on despite official injunctions.

To be sure, government was not alone in its concerns. In his recent book, *Soros on Soros*, the speculative genius and philanthropist writes:

> Popper maintained that the same methods and criteria apply to both social and natural science. He called this the doctrine of the unity of method. I have some doubts about this doctrine. I expressed them in the title of my book, *The Alchemy of Finance*. I argued that the expression 'social science'

is a false metaphor and reflexive events cannot be explained and predicted by universally applicable laws.

Perhaps our hosts today should have been called The Social Alchemy Council. But, then, George Soros is not only a graduate of the London School of Economics but was a student of Popper's so that he is, to his credit, able to go on to say:

> I now believe that I carried my arguments too far. It is possible to apply the methods and criteria of natural science to social phenomena and they may produce worthwhile results within their terms of reference.

The temptation is great to continue along such partly political, partly philosophical lines; but I shall resist it. My objective in this lecture is to develop one idea, one project almost, and to use the history of the London School of Economics to do so. The idea is that there remains a common theme for a science of human society and that while much progress has been made in developing its various facets and aspects, it is still important to try to tie the parts together – not in search of a 'world formula', such as has tempted the alchemists of natural science from time to time, but to make sense of the social habitat in which we live, have lived and are likely to live.

The century which followed the publication of the *Wealth of Nations* saw a rich flowering of social science all over Europe, and later in America as well. Smith's Scottish colleagues – Adam Ferguson, John Millar – extended the new methods into sociology. His own discipline bred ever new approaches to political and economic subjects: Ricardo and Malthus, Condorcet and Saint-Simon, Marx and List. Great system builders entered the scene: Comte, Spencer. Statistics evolved into social research, the first censuses, Henry Mayhew's studies of *London Labour and the London Poor*, Charles Booth's maps of inequality. Cities and revolutions, suicide and industry, peasants and engineers became subjects of social inquiry. How rich the nineteenth century was in new beginnings!

Yet, if we consider the nineteenth-century beginnings of social science in the light of David Hume's hopes, two things stand out. One is that the science of man, even in its most 'experimental' variants, was not cumulative. Emma Rothschild has recently made the point for economics, indeed for the economics of Adam Smith. It gave rise to two quite different traditions, one utilitarian and one institutional. The former assumed human beings were motivated by fear and greed, the latter by well-being; one ended with Milton Friedman and James Buchanan, the other with John Kenneth Galbraith, Albert Hirschman and Amartya Sen; one with Margaret Thatcher, the other with Jacques Delors. The examples point to the second marked feature of early social science, which is premature application. Knowledge for the sake of knowledge almost never existed. Science was from the beginning the 'science of a statesman or legislator'. A certain impatience accompanied even the beginnings of social science.

This is not to say that there was no progress. The giants of the nineteenth century showed an understanding of things social, unthinkable a century before – the German Freiherr von Stein, the Frenchman Alexis de Tocqueville, the Scotsman Sir James George Frazer. Then, at the turn of the century, there were the heroes of modern social science: Emile Durkheim, Vilfredo Pareto, Max Weber.

There was also the London School of Economics and Political Science. Its founders did not have a theory of the science of man; in fact, they were both rather untheoretical by temperament. Sidney Webb liked the idea of wanting to know the causes of things, but essentially in order to inform administrators of a fairer, a more just society. The École des Sciences Politiques and also the ideals of the Imperial German Social Democracy – a bit of Bismarck, a bit of Bebel, or better, Lassalle – were his models. W.A.S. Hewins, the other founder, had, at the tender age of 21, started a Social Science Club at Oxford designed 'to find a way to the solutions of social difficulties by practical investigation'. Experimental science it was, but hardly abstract, let alone theoretical.

However, the LSE which the two men built soon turned out to be a laboratory of the social sciences. It marks a phase in the history of this branch of knowledge which was present elsewhere too, though perhaps nowhere as tangible as at the young LSE. One might describe it as many windows looking out on the same landscape or, better perhaps, the same cityscape given the peculiarly modern bias of the social sciences. The lecturers of the early years each had their own style. The tall, imperious Halford Mackinder brought maps of the world, and notably of the 'heartland' of his geopolitics, East Central Europe, to life by combining history, sociology and economics with geography. W.A.S. Hewins himself oscillated between history, economics and politics without ever thinking about separate disciplines. Graham Wallas delved into psychology in order to teach politics, but never tried to identify the boundaries to economics, let alone sociology. Edwin Cannan, despite his own pedantic ways, did not share Alfred Marshall's disciplinary *amour propre* which is why, even against his intentions, he turned the early School into a home for German-style historical economists rather than theorists. L.T. Hobhouse subsumed it all in his grand evolutionary schemes, which transcended all boundaries in any case. No Thomas Kuhn here! No proprietary interest in paradigms and scientific communities! Since there were no disciplinary degree courses, no graduate assistants bent on their own advancement, no departmental labels either, one must envy the early students of LSE.

The notion of windows on the same sight, whether city or country, is meant quite seriously. The early social scientists did not doubt that they had one subject of inquiry. It looked a bit different from one angle than from the other, but it was still the same subject. They also did not doubt that they were trying to make sense of it. Whether they described or counted, looked into antecedents or connections, they wanted to understand the way people live together. Moreover, they wanted to understand it in order to change it. *Rerum cognoscere causas* was not the sole, and for many not the dominant motive of social science. 'Happy are those engaged in deliberately changing things!' would have been a more appropriate motto. Deliberate change meant, of course, intervention; intervention meant planning by experts. The anti-Gladstonian bias in the LSE foundation was also an anti-liberal bias. In retrospect this may look like socialism, but in fact it incorporated many elements above and beyond what we now call the welfare state, including the 'Efficiency Movement' of Rosebery, Webb's and others' French dream of public administration, and even the near-universal turn-of-the-century belief in eugenics, in breeding a better race of humans.

To be sure, this is not the whole truth of social science at the turn of the century. I have mentioned the heroes already: Emile Durkheim, Vilfredo Pareto, Max Weber; Alfred Marshall must be added to the list. None of them – and no one of similar stature – taught at the early LSE. They also had political predilections and in some cases, passions; but their scholarship remained in a certain sense pure. They were happy to concentrate on discovering the causes of things. But, for them too, social science was all of one piece. Alfred Marshall gave the lecture which led his (unrelated) namesake, T.H. Marshall, 65 years later to produce the brilliant *Citizenship and Social Class*. Pareto, the theorist of circulation of elites, became one of the fathers of formal economics. Max Weber's *Economy and Society* has become a rich quarry for historians and political scientists, as well as sociologists and, more sparingly, economists.

But such disciplinary labels tell a story of change. In the 1920s and 1930s the unity of social science fell apart. The social sciences in the plural emerged and before long some of those who had been present at the foundation, notably economists, would hesitate to call themselves social scientists at all. At LSE Lionel Robbins' *Essay on the Nature and Significance of Economic Science* marked an important departure. One notes the expression, 'economic science'. Others were quick to respond. In my *LSE* I have devoted sections to a number of parallel developments: Bowley and Social Statistics, Robbins and Economics, Laski and Political Science, Tawney and Economic History,

Malinowski and Anthropology, and then the unhappy episode of Hogben and Social Biology.

Hogben's clearly was a bridge too far, though he was neither the first nor the last to try to cross it. The point at issue here is, in any case, another one. After the initial phase of several windows on the same landscape, in a second phase a process of structuration took place. The social sciences cut up the landscape and found a series of different aspects – shapes of windows and kinds of lighting – to gaze at their specific segment. This was an exciting and in many ways desirable development which furthered the advancement of knowledge. It was also the source of rigidities and departmental parochialisms which were to weaken the social sciences a generation later.

Let me begin with the up-side. Economic science, already rich in historical antecedents, began a triumphant journey of discovery. Defined as the science of scarcity, it invited probability analysis, quantification and formalisation more generally, and soon models which took the place of an all-too-complex reality (though they remained useful for predicting real events). After Keynes – and in some ways with Keynes – it emigrated to the United States. Other social sciences followed. Social statistics became the seed corn not just of national accounting but also of social research. Techniques of research found many applications. By contrast, both economic history and anthropology seemed initially more 'qualitative' subjects, 'experimental' in the classical sense perhaps, that is, distinctly empirical, but bent on understanding complex processes rather than simplifying them for the sake of formal precision.

Sociology and political science did not easily find their place in this scheme of things. In a sense, 'political *science*' never really came to fruition in Britain. The Oxford tradition of PPE – politics, philosophy, economics – sustained the Oxford view of P, which was political theory, political philosophy perhaps. At LSE it entered into an uneasy alliance with public administration, or the study of government. Political science proper – in Lasswell's words: *Who Gets What, When, How?* – became a German (soon *émigré* German) and American discipline. Such developments raise intriguing questions of what was once called the 'sociology of knowledge'.

Sociology in turn went in a number of tenuously connected directions. Again, it is instructive to look at LSE. In an important period, there were three protagonists: the evolutionary philosopher Morris Ginsberg, the incisive social analyst T.H. Marshall, the master of empirical social research David Glass, plus for a while the *Diagnosis of our Time* author, and inventor of the 'sociology of knowledge', Karl Mannheim. If we add to them the names of the younger teachers of, say, 1950 – Jean Floud and Donald MacRae, Tom Bottomore and Julius Gould, Ernest Gellner and Robert McKenzie – we find a confusing mixture of Marx and anti-Marx, anthropology and history, description and prescription. Some of us who wrote our PhDs at the School in the early 1950s turned away from confusion and tried to define our own sociology of empirical macroanalysis.

The structuration of the social sciences had many facets. They all have this in common, that both the unity of method and the unity of subject matter were lost. *Homo oeconomicus*, the optimiser of well-being, had little in common with 'Malinowskian' man of reciprocal relations or, indeed, with *homo sociologicus*, the player of roles. Students of politics ceased to be able to read economic journals, and economists spurned sociological journals and books. Characteristically, the LSE BSc. (Econ), once built around a core of common subjects, came to be splintered into so many options that it was possible to get an economics degree without any economics at all. However, such excesses must not detract from the rich harvest of scholarly work and the equally rich variety of teaching offered in social science courses. The period of structuration was one of excitement and achievement. It was also one in which application was no longer as central as in the early phase. Social scientists found jobs not just in the expanding universities, but quite often applied research jobs in economic analysis or urban planning or survey research, rather than vantage points for creating the good society.

Older members of LSE like to point to the fact that the School has introduced departments as organised units later than most. This is true in the sense that there were, right up to the 1960s, no chairmen or convenors of departments, and both the Appointments Committee and the Academic Board maintained the fiction of a single faculty, indeed a single department school. But a fiction it was. No one would have confounded Lionel Robbins' concerns with those of Bronislaw Malinowski or Harold Laski. Subjects of scholarship, disciplines were increasingly clearly delineated. In the end it was only a small step for full-fledged departments to emerge, have their convenors, their departmental staff, their meetings and their distinctive claims on resources as well as recognition.

It is elementary sociology to predict that the process of structuration experienced by the social sciences in the 1920s and 1930s would harden into institutional structures with recognised boundaries and specific cultures. It did. When the great trade union theorist of science, Thomas Kuhn, presented the results of 15 years' hard thinking in 1962 (*The Structure of Scientific Revolutions*), he merely gave legitimacy to a process already complete in the natural and the social sciences, and in the humanities as well: there are 'scientific communities' and they have their 'paradigms'. 'A paradigm is what the members of a scientific community share and, conversely, a scientific community consists of men who share a paradigm.' Small wonder that Kuhn became one of the most widely quoted, and praised, epistemological authors of the time. His is a wonderful ideology to justify the establishment of all kinds of 'sciences' from astronomy to hotel management and economics to parapsychology.

It is all too easy to make fun of the effect of a theory which lends itself to vulgarisation and abuse as Kuhn's does. Every doctoral student nowadays claims to have found a new 'paradigm' and the proliferation of departments is invariably justified by reference to the emergence of a new 'scientific community'. I have called this a trade union theory not to insult trade unions but to indicate that it has more to do with the organisation of interests than the objectives of scientific inquiry. Scientific communities gathered around the flagpole of their paradigm are more likely to get involved in demarcation disputes than to advance knowledge. The institutionalisation of science along Kuhnian lines has many unfortunate consequences. The late Karl Popper exposed some of them when he argued that in the natural sciences the process could become a positive impediment to research when it came to people or projects which do not fit. His ill-tempered correspondence with the Royal Society about unrecognised research designs will no doubt emerge in due course. In the social sciences two consequences of the vulgarised Kuhn are particularly serious.

The first is that social science has lost its intrinsically public character. All sciences are public in intent, but if anything it is even more true of the social sciences that their findings need to be widely understood and openly debated. Scientific communities, on the other hand, have an apparently built-in tendency towards autarky. This is controlled in almost medieval ways, by guild-like rigidities and outright protectionism. Professional organisations control access, including access to academic jobs. Professional journals guard the paradigm(s). Whoever is not a part of the guild remains excluded. Worse, members acquire an unfortunate tendency to write for each other rather than for a more general public. The paradigm turns out to be a jargon adopted mainly in order to demonstrate who belongs and who does not. Perhaps this is, given the enormous expansion of the scientific community in the widest sense, the only protection against anomy, but in effect it destroys one of the basic values of (social) science: openness, and accessiblity, the public intent.

The other consequence of vulgarized Kuhn is, if anything, even more detrimental. For Kuhn, scientific communities are a necessary prerequisite of discoveries and the advancement of knowledge. Scientific communities are the 'producers and validators' of knowledge. But it could be argued that the guild-like nature of these communities can positively block new insights. Economists only see what their paradigms allow them to see; sociologists dismiss explanations because they are not sociological. This does no harm to the practitioners of disciplines; they are simply behaving as good members of their communities. On the other hand it impedes the advancement of science. Paradigms become narrow-vision looking-glasses which miss a wide range of phenomena.

All sciences are affected by these twin dangers, but it is safe to assume that disciplines worried about their status are more likely to fall victim than older and more confident ones. Thus the language of paradigms and scientific communities is particularly pernicious in many of the social sciences. It has already led to a combination of obtuseness and barrenness in important areas of economic and social research. The question is: how can we open up the social sciences again for new horizons? Whither social science after the initial burst of enthusiastic discoveries and the later process of structuration and institutionalization?

The question is not exactly new – nor would I make any such claim for the analysis offered here – and we can therefore consider real developments to answer it rather than engage in abstract prescription. The first remedy against the limitations of scientific communities which has been fashionable for some time, is interdisciplinary research. The principle is surely right: artificial boundaries between disciplines must not impede knowledge. Whatever people's disciplinary passport, they have to cross boundaries. However, the risk is great that interdisciplinary research, instead of abolishing borders, in fact hardens them. Scholars enter into negotiations about arrangements resembling treaties between sovereign states: I provide the economic perspective, and you the sociological one ... In the end the paradigms are all confirmed and the boys have all found jobs, but knowledge is not advanced. Interdisciplinary work is therefore popular among scholars but does not solve the more serious problems discussed here.

At the other end of the scale of remedies there are attempts to bridge all gaps and cross all borders by a kind of synthetic social super-science. Again, it would be wrong to deprecate good intentions. It is, however, a fact that recent attempts to integrate all social sciences into one comprehensive systematic approach have failed. Take Talcott Parsons. He set out (in *The Structure of Social Action*) with a thorough analysis of the heroes. He then proceeded (in *The Social System*, and before that in *Toward a General Theory of Action*) to develop categories which apply to all events and processes in the purview of social science. To prove the point, Parsons went on to apply his approach to the economy (*Economy and Society*) and also to religion, to class, in short to the whole gamut of Max Weber's far-flung concerns. But nobody listened. A few sociologists did, but even anthropologists shied away and economists, or historians, took no notice at all. Why? Why is this also the case for other synthesizers like Jürgen Habermas or Niklas Luhmann or Anthony Giddens?

Perhaps the attempt is overambitious and even unnecessary. Just as Werner Heisenberg and Carl Friedrich von Weizsäcker did not advance science by their attempts at a super-science, so the social super-scientists remain irrelevant. Perhaps it is also suspicious that so many of them are sociologists. They are seen as trying to overcome disciplinary rigidities by the imperialism of one discipline. They are of course not alone in this attempt. Economists in particular have at times felt that there is no real need for other social sciences because they can tackle any subject that comes their way. Kenneth Arrow's disciple Anthony Downs provided a good example with his *Economic Theory of Democracy* (though more recent attempts by the Virginia School, James Buchanan, Gordon Tullock, are even more ambitious). Again, the assault on the world of disciplines, of social-scientific communities has failed. The perspective of economics is too limited after all. Votes are not like dollars; there are institutions to determine the political process, parties, classes and all. Exit is only one response (to quote a great political economist), there is also voice and loyalty.

This last comment takes us straight to one of the more hopeful recent developments in the social sciences, the emergence of disciplines which without any grand design manage to tackle problems with the entire armoury created by the various scientific communities. Three such developments stand out. One is associated with Albert Hirschman as much as anybody; it is *political economy*. The revival of political economy is one of the remarkable phenomena of these years. It occurs from two directions. On the one hand there are economists who transcend the narrow boundaries of their community and rediscover institutions. It was gratifying to encounter several of them at LSE in my time; Amartya Sen, of course, and Partha Dasgupta, Tony Atkinson and Nicholas Barr. On the other hand there are political scientists who begin to realize that their analyses lack bottom if they do not incorporate economic analysis. In the United States the subject of the future of the welfare state has attracted the interest of political scientists who in the process have rediscovered classical political economy.

Two other social sciences come to mind as one looks for hopeful new departures beyond the narrow paradigms of departmental communities. One is *economic history*. It was throughout the history of the social sciences a subject of transdisciplinary interest; the great debate about religion and the rise of capitalism is but one example. More recently, however, a number of economic historians have achieved the almost impossible, which is to integrate econometrics and even some economic theory into historical analysis. The 1993 Nobel Prize for Robert Fogel and Douglass North gave much encouragement to this intellectual venture, though one must hope that it will not too soon be frozen into a paradigm around which another hermetic scientific community forms.

Then there is *social anthropology*. Ever since it has run out of tribes it has stimulated the systematic and comprehensive analysis of modern communities. Like economic historians, social anthropologists have remained unperturbed by the disciplinary origins of their perspectives. As a result they have enriched our understanding of economic cultures and socio-political behaviour significantly.

This in fact is the key to progress in the social sciences today: disrespect for the proprietary claims of existing scientific communities. Science is about problems and problems do not belong to anybody, not even to the guilds of economists or political scientists. Even less do the perspectives brought to bear on their solution belong to the defenders of particular paradigms. The ESRC now likes to speak of 'themes' which encapsulate the 'broad priorities for the future social science research agenda'. This is a step in the right direction, although of course a Research Council has to 'allow all social science disciplines to continue their distinctive contributions', and a Research Council in present-day Britain has to make the risky promise of a contribution to the needs of users, the competitiveness of the economy, the quality of life and the effectiveness of public services. I call it a risky promise, because no one can know whether research will deliver such goods, and the harder it tries to do so the less likely it is to succeed. It is better to aim at pure research and then be surprised by its applications than to start with practical intentions and then produce hasty and shoddy results. But themes, or as I prefer to say, problems, are the right beginning, and of course problems should be related to questions which the condition of economy and society around us poses.

The question which I find most vexing these days and which I must therefore leave unanswered, is: where will the next steps forward in the social sciences take place? What is the right environment, what is the institutional framework for discovery and innovation? My attachment to LSE is no secret and has become evident again in this lecture. Sometimes when I am asked to define the social sciences, I simply say, LSE. The School provides what was long a unique framework for research and teaching in all social sciences, and its slightly shambolic appearance contributes to making the ossification of scientific communities less likely. But, like all universities, LSE has grown and been forced by unwanted pressures to dissipate its original purposes. Sometimes I wonder whether universities as we knew them are still 'where it's at' as we approach the new century.

Here I have a confession to make. In writing my *LSE* I produced two versions of the final, brief section which in the published version is entitled 'Past and Future'. The point of these pages now is that past strengths will see the School through present challenges. We cannot know yet how exactly this will happen and where exactly it will lead, but we can be confident of a strong institution finding its way. This I believe; otherwise I would not have said so. But the earlier version emphasized questions and doubts. Are universities among the great achievements of the twentieth century which the twenty-first is not going to see? Has (*pace* Popper) the world spirit moved on to other parts of the universe of institutions? Have London, a school of learning, economics, and political science all become exhausted and outdated experiences?

I was sufficiently self-critical to shelve such questions as products of a nostalgia that comes with advancing age. But questions remain even if one discounts such disabilities. Britain now has a number of vibrant policy research institutes. When it comes to application they are probably at least as useful and effective as any university. Curiously, these institutes are called 'think tanks', when in fact they are action-oriented, indeed geared to precisely the objectives which the ESRC is now associating with its 'themes': 'enhancing the UK's economic competitiveness, quality of life and the effectiveness of its public services'. But what Britain does not have is an institute of advanced study in which knowledge – notably in the social sciences – is cultivated for knowledge's sake.

Actually, Britain is almost alone in this deficiency. The US have Princeton and Palo Alto and the National Endowment for the Humanities. In France almost everything is an institute of advanced study, especially if it is called a school, like the École d'Hautes Études. Germany has the Berlin Wissenschaftskolleg, Holland the Wassenaar Institute, Austria the Institute of Human Sciences. Even in Eastern Europe such centres begin to flourish. How did David Hume put it? 'Nor ought we to think, that this latter improvement in the science of man will do less honour to our native country than the former in natural philosophy ...' Arguably the greater need today is for a place of sheer excellence than for one of premature application.

11   The Public Responsibility of Intellectuals: Against the New Fear of the Enlightenment

Lionel Trilling Seminar Lecture, given at Columbia University, New York, on 27 January 1994

What I want to say in introducing this Lionel Trilling Seminar is simple, probably too simple for a spoilt post-modern audience: Intellectuals have a public responsibility. Where they remain silent, societies have lost their future. Intellectuals may or may not wish to take sides in partisan argument, though if they all huddle together on one side, something has gone wrong. It is the responsibility of intellectuals to speak up and thereby address those involved in the trials and tribulations of active life. At the end of the twentieth century, the Enlightenment compact between ideas and actions may have lost some of its charm, but it has lost none of its strength as a force for freedom.

Making the case for this thesis is, however, far from simple. After two or three attempts I have given up all hope of being able to make it systematically. In the end I decided to stop trying and to talk instead about five people who have something to tell us about the subject, and in each case single out one aspect of their thought: Karl Popper, Josef König, Jürgen Habermas, Edward Said, Ernest Gellner. If what I have to say about them does not add up to a consistent argument, I must ask your indulgence. At the very least, a stance may shine through which informs the view of one intellectual who still wants to persuade others of 'the uniqueness of truth' without trusting anyone who claims to possess it.

KARL POPPER

In the course of recent visits to the nonagenarian philosopher in his bungalow in Surrey, just inside the M25, the motorway ring around London, conversation would invariably turn to one of two subjects: great scandals which he has uncovered, or his own reputation in the world. The scandals are, on reflection, all of one kind. They are about the public responsibility of the scientist.

For a year, if not more, Popper kept on his desk a pile of mostly big books relating to the Cuban missile crisis. Andrej Sacharow's *Memoirs* provided the key to his own interest. Years ago, Popper had praised the Russian physicist and dissident on the occasion of the award of the Freedom Prize. Now he had discovered to his dismay that Sacharow was in fact (as Popper insists on claiming) a 'war criminal'. He had not only contributed to producing the Soviet nuclear capacity, but advised Krushchev to install missiles in Cuba and, if necessary, use them against the United States. Sacharow himself had admitted as much. Popper desperately wanted to undo his earlier praise for the man, and was angry that no one except the Italian Communist newspaper *Unitá* would listen to him, angry even with me for wondering how there can be a war criminal without a war. 'But it was a war, and it was won by the United States of America.'

On another occasion (and here my own ignorance of the subject in question makes the story of necessity a little vague) the great man showed me a letter from the President of the Royal Society. Popper had received a research proposal from a young Indian scientist who lacked the facilities for a crucial experiment in, I think, biophysics. Popper had asked the Royal Society (of which he is a Fellow) to provide the facilities, but the response was, as expected, that this could not be done because no one had ever heard of the young Indian. Popper was outraged, but failed to persuade the establishment of the need for more openness. Science had become 'a sham', he would say, adding more tellingly that it showed more and more signs of a rigid guild in which esoteric games are played which betray the underlying values of the great enterprise of science. Science has destroyed its own foundations.

This is where the second regular subject of conversation comes in, Popper's own position. Partly this is a grand old man speaking who, despite his frequent travels and uncounted prizes and honorary degrees, feels out of things; Popper complains that he has been forgotten. Once he told me that he had looked up an annual list of dissertations written in the United States, and found only a handful about his work. But there was also a grain of truth. Contrary to the view of admirers of *The Open Society* and *The Poverty of Historicism*, Popper sees himself primarily as a scientist. In recent years, he has published half a dozen books on quantum mechanics, astronomy, and, of course, biology. But the scientific community has largely ignored him, or so he believes.

Popper is, above all, a great public scientist. He belongs to that small band of which Albert Einstein is the founder and patron in this century. (Popper actually likes to describe himself as 'a nineteenth-century scientist'.) Public scientists have made seminal contributions to knowledge but have also insisted that knowledge must, in principle, be accessible. They feel a responsibility which extends far beyond the circle of their colleagues. They may at times be hard to understand, but are never intentionally esoteric. It follows from this attitude that they do not confine themselves to concern with the logic of scientific discovery; they are equally committed to what may be called the ethic of scientific discovery, and indeed the moral consequences of science. Thus, they try to keep that noble human activity, scientific enquiry, within the bounds of ordinary life; they are and want to be seen to be members of society at large.

'Scientific community' may well be the operative word in this context. Thomas Kuhn, and even more so the vulgarizers of *The Structure of Scientific Revolutions*, have a lot to answer for. The book and the name of its author have become the charter and founding father of a kind of trade unionism in science. Closed shops which exclude unknown young Indian biophysicists provide a comfortable home for those who are inside. The inmates play their own little games. Every now and again someone is credited with having invented a new 'paradigm' which puts him or her a few notches up in the citation index, and gives them promotion, but all this takes place without anyone outside the charmed circle taking any notice. 'Scientific communities' are largely about themselves. Biophysicists talk to biophysicists, political scientists to political scientists, and even historians – once the guardians and protagonists of public scholarship – have acquired a habit of playing their private games of revision and reconstruction.

When I was first appointed to a chair 37 years ago, I still had the oldfashioned title of a *professor ordinarius publicus*. I am not entirely sure where the 'public' in the title came from. Perhaps it was meant to contrast with the miseries of that other, junior and unpaid status, the *Privatdozent*. Possibly some polite hint was intended at the fact that the funding of professors, in Europe at least, came and still comes largely from the public purse. But there was also the obligation to give lectures in public. ('Publish or perish' was not yet a maxim of academic culture.) Scholars were, as they should be, men and women of the mind who advance and disseminate knowledge.

There is a difficulty here which must not go unnoticed. The process of scientific discovery, and of scholarship generally, requires a protected space. Knowledge is not advanced in the marketplace. The autonomy of universities is an essential condition, as is the availability of time, indeed in principle of unlimited time. If real time begins to invade academic time, as by financial exigencies and bureaucratic requirements, the quality of scholarship suffers. In that sense, science and scholarship need their own institutions, perhaps even including scientific communities around certain areas of enquiry. But the role, the task and the duty of the scholar cannot be defined by the boundaries of the world of scholarship. If science may be said to be 'private' in a literal and oldfashioned sense of the word, that is, removed from the grasp of public interest, the scientist is not – and the scientist and the scholar may be taken as both metaphors and examples for the intellectual.

JOSEF KÖNIG

Perhaps, a second encounter, that with my teacher in philosophy many years ago at the University of Hamburg, can help us make more sense of such hunches and suggestions. Josef König (who was never well-known beyond the confines of the German language) tried the impossible, which was to use the analysis of language in order to develop moral conclusions. Thus he fell between the Oxford fad of linguistic philosophy, and older as well as newer attempts to approach issues of moral philosophy directly. In the process, König conveyed to his students both the rigour of analysis and the painful pleasures of commitment, *engagement* as it was called in those existentialist days.

König liked to make a point which is relevant to Popper's notion of the activity of science. He distinguished between what he called 'questions' posed by life itself, and 'problems' made up by us, and notably by scientists. We cannot avoid answering questions even if we do not give an answer; abstention is a vote too. We can, on the other hand, avoid solving problems; nothing happens if we quietly forget about them. The professor who goes to a committee meeting is answering a question, perhaps that of who should get how much money for research. While he or she is whiling away the hours in a committee tug-of-war, his or her problem, the next conjecture in a corrupted classical text, the next experiment in exploring the causes of migraine, remains unattended in the study or the laboratory, and nothing happens as a result. The distinction is subtle and important. It has much to do with real time and academic time, and even with the vexing problem (or is it a question?) of the morality of everyday life and the morality of scientific enquiry. Suffice it to suggest, in the present context, that there is something to be said for problems which have some relation to questions. The public scholar or scientist may well be, and in some sense should be, stimulated by questions which life has posed, his or her own life, but also the lives of others. There is certainly nothing wrong with using our minds in order to try and improve the human condition.

But the reason why I wanted to turn to Josef König is a different one. I have written about it in my contribution to the volume on *Science and Social Structure* edited in 1980 by Thomas F. Gieryn for the New York Academy of Sciences in honour of one of the great Columbia professors of our time,

Robert K. Merton. The piece is entitled, 'Representative Activities', and revolves around a moving and profound statement by Josef König in a letter written in 1953. Philosophy and art as activities are not simply hobbies like playing football or collecting stamps (König says). They are activities with some 'general validity'. He, König, always saw something incongruous and embarrassing in being paid for engaging in such an activity; a feeling not shared by many latter-day public professors. 'It makes no sense, or so it seems to me, to say for example: he who plays football, or collects stamps, is doing this *representatively* for all others. But for being a philosopher, or an artist, this strange "representative" quality might be valid on the understanding that only he does it in the right manner who does it "representatively".' This 'right manner' has something to do with observing rules, and also with not being too certain that one acts in a representative manner.

In the contribution to the Merton *Festschrift*, I have briefly traced the moral ambiguities of this idea in the light of its history from Aristotle's 'theoretical life' for free men to Hegel's and Marx's hidden alliance with the World Spirit and on to Nietzsche's *Übermensch*. I also referred to more recent and more plausible versions of the notion of representative activities: Max Weber's 'vocations' of science and of politics; Albert Camus' 'vocation' of the artist 'to open the prisons and to give a voice to the sorrows and joys of all', Popper's curiously named 'World 3' of 'abstract but nonetheless real' products of the mind which 'are powerful tools for changing World 1', the real, physical world. Edward Said, in his Reith Lectures to which I shall return, toys and plays with the notion of 'representations' and then finds himself saying: 'The intellectual is an individual endowed with a faculty for representing, embodying, articulating a message, a view, an attitude, philosophy or opinion to, as well as for, a public, in public.'

The risk of an unbearable arrogance is evident as one is making such statements. This risk made me quote Josef König, who was notably free of believing that special faculties gave him special entitlements. But the question remains (and it is a question rather than a problem): why are we here tonight? Some perhaps wish they were not. For others it may be a sense of duty. Few, if any, have come for financial gain, and that includes the lecturer. Many, I hope, came for fun in the best sense of the word. But all these are incidental reasons. Above all, we have come to explore important problems together. They are important because we define them as such, and also because they have to do with questions of our own lives and their meaning.

So why do we want to know the causes of things and speak about our discoveries? *Felix qui potuit rerum cognoscere causas*, but happiness is not all. We feel that since we can, we must; since we are able to engage in the attempt to make sense of the world around us, it is our duty to do so. In a 'politically correct' world such statements may seem offensive to some; they define philosophers and artists as having a public responsibility yet being not just members of the public. However, the duty to do what one is able to do on behalf of others who are unable or unwilling to do it is an eminently moral precept, as long as it is bound by rules which are transparent and allow accountability.

JÜRGEN HABERMAS

Such reflections do not answer the question: whom do intellectuals represent? What exactly is, in other words, the constituency of those who speak for, or on behalf of, others? Karl Mannheim has argued persuasively in his *Ideology and Utopia* that the groups from which they come, and above all their classes of origin, are not the constituency of intellectuals. Intellectuals have broken with their 'normal' allegiances, they are socially 'free-floating'. Even if they are claimed by particular groups, or indeed try to please them, this is not done naively. The absence of naive class or other group interest is a defining characteristic of intellectuals. Intellectuals represent the public in a more diffuse but also more inclusive sense.

But what is this public? In his first book, Jürgen Habermas has traced the 'structural change of the public' in the sense of the old marketplace of those who have a sense of responsibility for the *res publica* and the wherewithal to express it. The public of Locke, and of Burke, and even of Mill, is no longer. Sometimes one wonders whether even 'the people' in the old emphatic sense, *le peuple*, *das Volk* have ceased to exist. What could it mean nowadays that someone is 'a man (or woman) of the people'? The great destructuring process of the century has torn up the textures which could be regarded as given in earlier times. Brief crystallizations of individual elements have taken the place of structures of region, religion and class. Now you see society and now you don't, to say nothing of 'public opinion'. Intellectuals have always been rootless but in the past they did not lack a constituency to which their words were addressed. Perhaps it is not surprising that in the absence of such a constituency they increasingly talk to each other.

From one point of view, the constituency which takes the place of the old public is the lifelong subject of Jürgen Habermas's theories. He wants to recreate society without reintroducing old constraints. The medium of this recreation is language, the instrument, discourse. New norms are generated by unconstrained discourse. Who engages in it? The logic of Habermas's argument must lead him to some notion of community. He likes the word, *naturwüchsig*, naturally grown and growing, not closed to be sure, but bonded. The 'communitarianism' which seems to occupy the language of the left at the end of this century as 'collectivism' did at its beginning – in both cases a protest against exaggerated individualism – has something to do with the search for a constituency. Creating communities of discourse is almost a matter of survival for representatives without represented.

In the meantime, most intellectuals rely on more real and also more lucrative means of survival, in particular the media. Mass media with their often unknown and always invisible audience are the appropriate means of communication in societies without class, status and party. They enable intellectuals to speak without giving much thought to their constituency. In fact the diffuseness of the constituency allows representations without responsibility. Under such circumstances, opinionizing if not philosophizing becomes a hobby after all, talkshow entertainment rather than representative activity.

This is not all of course. Habermas himself is very much a public professor. It could be said perhaps that his frequent utterances about contemporary issues bear little relation to his complex and highly esoteric theories, but his reputation as a scholar give his pleas for 'constitutional patriotism' or against '*deutschmark* nationalism' added weight. In fact, he has done better than others in his country when the public responsibility of German intellectuals was challenged in recent years. The story would warrant a lecture of its own. German unification has revealed just how deeply most intellectuals had become attached to the cosy world of the old Federal Republic of Germany, protected by a wall and 'another country' to the east and by a French Europe and an American Atlantic alliance to the west. This state of affairs could be criticised to one's heart's delight without any threat to its continued existence or risk to the critic. Now that it has collapsed, and at least in Germany not collapsed through any intellectual activity à la Havel or Michnik, the familiar names around *Die Zeit* in Hamburg, to say nothing of Günther Grass, are perplexed and filled with nostalgia. Jürgen Habermas is not entirely free of such sentiments, though he is at least trying to come to terms with his new constituency.

His constituency after all? Community, social cohesion is undoubtedly important. It is for good reason a lively subject of debate among those who seek more life chances for more people. But the new public will not arise from civil society alone. Indeed, even civil society does not exist without structures of power. If we wait for *naturwüchsig* processes to do the job of identifying where we belong and thus for whom we speak, we may well end up in Bosnia. I suspect that the constituency for the representative activities of intellectuals is both the real public of existing political communities, among which the heterogeneous nation-state is still the most civilized, and the imagined public which is the modern counterpart of the Swiss *Landesgemeinde* assembled on Sunday morning in a real marketplace for its solemn deliberation.

EDWARD SAID

In his 1993 Reith Lectures on *Intellectuals* Edward Said strides boldly over the ground into which I am tiptoeing in this lecture. In his own allusive and ironic style he has much to say about the representative functions of intellectuals, their public responsibility, their critical detachment and the dangers of professionalism. The notion of a constituency holds special pitfalls for him, the Palestinian in the West whose nation exists and yet does not exist even now. He might well argue against some of the reflections offered here by saying that the intellectual does not represent any particular group ever, and if he does he is likely to stray from the path of critical detachment. 'Speaking truth to power' is the ultimate public responsibility of intellectuals. 'In the end one is moved by causes and ideas that one can actually choose to support because they conform to values and principles one believes in.' Intellectuals have addressees, those in power, but their 'constituency' is in the last analysis not any social group, but the truth of these values and principles alone.

If I were to take issue with Said (and as a former Reith Lecturer myself, I must, of course, not do any such thing), I would probably start with the curious even-handedness of his criticism. Said appears to argue against the relativism of a world in which universals are almost completely absent, but he responds to it by putting all sides in the wrong in equal measure. Iraq should not have invaded Kuwait, but the West should not have gone to war against Iraq either. Khomeini's absolute claims are untenable, but his critics have mistakenly sanctified Western values. (One of the most worrying intellectual lives of our days, Salman Rushdie, does not appear in this context.) Said manages to achieve a near-total detachment from almost everything; even as a Member of the Palestine National Council he maintained what he calls, 'these perhaps too protestant positions of mine'. 'I refused all offers to occupy official positions; I never joined any party or faction.' Of course he did not 'join the Israeli or American side', but he also 'never endorsed the policies of, or even accepted official invitations from, Arab states'. To what then, if anything, is the intellectual committed?

In the third of his six lectures, Edward Said speaks at some length of Theodor W. Adorno who for him is 'the dominating intellectual conscience of the middle 20th century', 'a forbidding but endlessly fascinating man whose entire career skirted and fought the dangers of fascism, Communism and Western mass consumerism'. One has to repeat the triad of conjoined evils: fascism, communism, Western mass consumerism. Said describes Adorno's life as a sequence of unhappy encounters: the Nazi's seizure of power, Oxford positivism, the detested vulgarity of America, and after the war, the Americanization of the world. 'Adorno was the quintessential intellectual, hating all systems, whether on our side or theirs, with equal distaste.' Said goes on quoting from the *Minima Moralia*, Adorno's ambitious collection of aphorisms. 'Dwelling, in the proper sense, is now impossible.' 'Wrong life cannot be lived rightly.' Said's third Reith Lecture is entitled 'Intellectual Exile', and Adorno for him was forever 'stamped with the marks of exile'.

Much, indeed all, of this is, of course, correct, and yet some of us remember a different Adorno. Adorno liked to celebrate alienation, his own and that of everyone else. An exile he was, but always in comfort. Not for him a last desperate trek across the Pyrenees; he was long safe in New York when his 'friend' Walter Benjamin took his own life at Port-Bou. Adorno enjoyed the great hotels, the *Waldhaus* in Flims, *Brenner's Park* in Baden-Baden, where he would jot down his aphorisms about the horror of American films and the consumption-addicted masses in supermarkets. Said says that Adorno hated all systems 'with equal distaste'. The word is well-chosen. Adorno's analyses are all essentially aesthetic. He resembles Carl Schmitt and, above all, Ernst Jünger on the right in his fundamentally, and deliberately a-moral judgements. Indeed, 'right' and 'left' are not words which properly describe this approach which is protected from the real world by a thick pane of glass which is resistant to gunfire but, above all, keeps the smells of reality out. For me, Adorno epitomizes what are called, in German, *Salonbolschewisten*, revolutionaries of the drawing room.

This is undoubtedly a possible intellectual posture. How could it not be since it is real? I quite enjoy reading authors like Theodor Adorno and Ernst Jünger, if only out of admiration for their *legerdemain* of language, their outrageous if opaque generalizations, the allusions which leave almost everything open. 'Dwelling, in the proper sense, is now impossible.' 'Wrong life cannot be lived rightly.' What is one to make of such statements except to chuckle about the cheats? The posture has its own logic: everything is so awful that I may as well have a good time. It is almost certainly not an enlightened posture in the traditional sense. The 'dialectics of enlightenment' has got stuck in negation. (*Negative Dialectics* is the appropriate title of one of Adorno's books.) The notion of public responsibility is entirely alien to this posture. How did Josef König put it? The philosopher engages in representative activity 'on the understanding that only he does it in the right manner who does it "representatively"', and, of course, only those who are not too sure of their own standing. Of his, Adorno never had any doubt, and he would have poured scorn over the moral implications of 'the right manner'.

ERNEST GELLNER

As I turn to the last of my witnesses I am less and less certain that their galaxy adds up to any conclusion, except that I find myself in large agreement with the philosopher-anthropologist Ernest Gellner. On Sunday, 31 May 1992, the agnostic Prague-born Jew gave a sermon in the chapel of King's College, Cambridge, on 'The Uniqueness of Truth'. In it, Gellner pursues the triangular contest, as he sees it, of modern attitudes to truth. 'The three ideological contestants on the current scene, as far as I can judge, are the Relativists, the Fundamentalists, and a group which, for lack of a better name, I shall call Enlightenment Puritans.' The three are locked in a hopeless struggle in which each can overcome the other, only to be overcome in turn, 'a little like the children's game of scissors, paper, stone: scissors cut paper, paper covers stone, stone blunts scissors'.

Gellner describes the two positions which are not his own with considerable understanding, though this is more evident in his treatment of fundamentalism than of relativism. The Relativists dominate the 'groves of academe' with their view that anything goes. All approaches to truth are equally valid, and have to be tolerated in their own right. Gellner approves of such toleration, but minds the 'affectation, insincerity, self-contradiction, hidden condescension' of Relativists, and boldly asserts: 'Our world is indeed a plural one, but it is based on the uniqueness of truth.' At this point he is thinking of modern science, though not of the philosophy of science, let alone that of moral behaviour. This is where the Fundamentalists come in who 'are not always considered as wholly suitable for polite society' but 'have a supremely important point: truth does matter. It is not multicoloured and meretricious, and at the beck and call of any optional angle of vision.' Thus 'the Fundamentalists have a point against the Relativists: you are not serious, you are not consistent, and your position cannot really endow anyone with genuine moral conviction'.

What about the Enlightenment Puritans then, the EPs as Gellner also calls them? They are above all 'just a little more fastidious in identifying that truth which deserves such respect'. Truth is unique, but it is not revealed; it has to be sought and may never be found. The search for truth is an unending quest, though one which treats all evidence on an equal footing. This approach 'does not warm the heart' which may be its weakness. 'The Fundamentalist and the Enlightenment Puritan share a sense of and respect for the uniqueness of truth; the EP and the Relativist, share a penchant for tolerance; and the Relativist and the Fundamentalist, share a reasonably well furnished, habitable world, as opposed to the arid emptiness of the world of the EP.' Why then be an EP?

Here Gellner's argument takes one of those twists for which he is justly famous. In the terms of this lecture, he suddenly and unexpectedly steps out of the world of problems and into that of questions. EP works; it has served us rather well, especially if we add 'a touch of fundamentalism [to] ensure that the mix is not so thin, so disembodied as to lose all moral suggestiveness'. This 'ambiguous, unstable, uneasy relationship between Faith, Indifference, and Seriousness' works in politics and also in moral life more generally. It is, of course, hard to construct deliberately, precisely because of its 'compromise ambiguity'. This is also why one hesitates and wonders as one recommends it to the new democracies of Eastern Europe, for example. And yet it is the only approach to truth which has ever offered people freedom and progress, growing life chances in open societies. We in the fortunate West should count our blessings.

I agree with the thrust of Gellner's sermon; and a sermon it is when at the critical point it turns to the evidence of our lives rather than the logic of discourse. Speaking of the uniqueness of truth is another way of saying that there are universal principles not just of knowledge but of morality too. However, we cannot ever be sure to have found them. We must, therefore, beware of fundamental dogmatism as much as of the *libertinage* of the relativist. It hardly needs saying that the intellectual, Ernest Gellner for example, has a very special place in such a scheme of things, reminding us all the time of the need for truth as well as that for toleration.

Where does all this take us? As I come to the end, I must disappoint you. For I shall do no more than repeat what I said at the beginning: Intellectuals have a public responsibility. Where they remain silent, societies have lost their future. Intellectuals may or may not wish to take sides in partisan argument, though if they all huddle together on one side, something has gone wrong. It is the responsibility of intellectuals to speak up and thereby address those involved in the trials and tribulations of active life. At the end of the twentieth century, the Enlightenment compact between ideas and actions may have lost some of its charm, but it has lost none of its strength as a force for freedom.

Britain, Germany
and Europe

12 Berlin for Example: From Zero Hour to Civil Society

Address on the occasion of the 50th anniversary of the end of the Second World War, organized by the City of Berlin at the Philharmonie on 21 April 1995

Zero hour lasted a long time fifty years ago. Its traces continue to linger in the memories of Germans. I am reminded of a clock which I have at home: every time the shelves of the cupboard on which it stands are opened, the whole clock is shaken up. Then the second hand performs strange acrobatics. It ticks on steadily from the 6 but hesitates as it approaches the 9, goes on ticking for a moment without actually advancing, drops back nearly to the 6, tries again, manages in the end to reach the 12 in tiny, painful steps, only to drop forward exhausted from the 12 by way of the 3 on to the 6. Like this somehow, not as a regular, let alone deliberate, rhythm of progress, Germany's path from the Zero Hour of 1945 to more happier recent times lives in my memory.

Here in Berlin the path was especially rich in pitfalls and obstacles. Ever new discouragements followed the encouragement of the first days of peace. I am thinking of the forced merger of Social Democrats and Communists in the Soviet Zone of Occupation, of the increasingly evident division of the city, the separate currency reforms, the blocking of access routes and the 'air bridge', the creation of two German states with Berlin in uncertain limbo, the East Berlin uprising of 17 June 1953 and in the end the Wall, that unforgettable monument of the fear of party bosses and of state terror.

Let us never forget that all this was the partly immediate, and partly remote consequence of a regime which Germans had voluntarily chosen and deliberately supported. To be sure, many realized too late the destructive linkages: Hitler's regime meant suppression within and aggression without. Both followed a dreadful spiral of acceleration, all the way to genocide within and war without. These in turn ended in a gigantic 'Jonestown', the megalomaniac suicide of a *Führer* who ordered his entire people to follow him into death.

If starting anew is to make any sense after such traumas and crimes, this must be about freedom – about liberal institutions, but also prosperity, and

125

above all about the anchor for both, civil society. Of these I want to speak in my address. And let me make one point clear right away: things German will not be cast in the gloomy light of crime and punishment. The keynote of my reflections on five chains of events in postwar Germany is hope. Germany has made as much of fifty years of peace as could possibly be achieved. I cannot think of another country which has made more decisive use of a new beginning like that of 1945 than the part of Germany which enjoyed the good fortune of freedom – and even the process of unification, with its inevitable mistakes and avoidable shortcomings of understanding and imagination, belongs ultimately on the credit side of Germany's balance of accomplishments. The reason for such success is above all that in these fifty years elements of a civil society have developed in the free Germany which alone guarantee a peaceful country. One must hope that its structures, habits and attitudes will maintain their strength in the united Germany and will further flourish.

But let us begin at the beginning, with Zero Hour. Those who have experienced it in Berlin, as I have, will not forget it. At the end of April the sound of artillery fire came closer and closer to the 'settlement' at the edge of the Grunewald forest in the district of Berlin with the absurd name, *Onkel Toms Hütte*, Uncle Tom's Cabin. I had hidden in the basement, ever since the surprising release from the prison camp in Schwetig near Frankfurt on Oder at the end of January. With me was a friend from our wartime refuge outside Berlin, who had managed to get stuck on his way to the army unit to which he was drafted. The women next door, who until recently had received a string of senior SS officers at all times of the day and night, were now hanging white sheets of another surrender outside their windows. Across the road (we learned later) the upright First World War veteran had shot dead first his wife and then himself because he could not bear the shame of defeat. The first Russian officers who came up our street spoke German. An hour later we hurriedly cut gaps into the garden fences behind the semi-detached houses so that women could get away through the back when Soviet soldiers demanded entry at the front door.

Zero Hour was a moment of complete anarchy, indeed anomy. No rule obtained, no authority existed. Arbitrariness – randomness really – could mean violence and often did, but it could also mean compassion and touching gestures, like that by the Soviet soldier on horseback who found a woman crying about the bicycle stolen by one of his comrades, and gave her his horse instead, thus leaving her totally perplexed. With others I went to the shopping arcade in the subway station of Onkel Toms Hütte. There was not much left to loot; even shelves and tables had been taken from shops; however, in the bookshop I found some volumes of romantic poetry which attracted the 16-year-old no less than potatoes and firewood.

The path from this Zero Hour to a new normality had two aspects. One came from above, from the Soviet Military Administration. I had a small part in it when I became first street supervisor in our 'settlement', then deputy head of food supplies for the borough of Zehlendorf. The all-important office, led by Enno Kind, a loveable photographer with a convenient Communist past, merely meant that we directed Soviet army lorries with oil, flour and meat from the yard of the local school to 22 distribution points in Zehlendorf. Moreover, it did not last very long; a few weeks later I found myself sitting in a classroom of the school instead of giving orders in its yard.

In any case, the other aspect is more important. If there is no state, no authority and no party either, one has to help oneself. Zero hour was the great hour of self-help. It is quite appropriate that a monument was later erected to the *Trümmerfrau*, the woman clearing up debris. She may have embodied a sad and suffering version of self-help, yet she is the precursor of the mature citizen. She is not waiting for Godot nor is she queuing at a counter but she gets her hands dirty doing things herself. Much later I encountered similar responses in places where great catastrophes had led to the complete collapse of the otherwise self-important authorities. In Mexico City, for example, the earthquake of 1985 led to the emergence of a kind of civil society. Suddenly all those initiatives sprang up from below which had so long been missing; there was even cooperation between groups. Anomy not only creates temptations of new tyranny but also chances of self-help activities of citizens.

Unfortunately, in Berlin the new tyranny was not long in coming either. I do not want to bore you with too many personal reminiscences but will add this one. Some time ago a friend who had looked up documents in the Central Party Archive of East Germany's Socialist Unity Party (SED) sent me a copy of a handwritten note by the Communist leader (later the first President of the GDR) Wilhelm Pieck, written on 25 February 1946. 'Gustav Dahrendorf [my father],' it said, 'to Hamburg, resigned from all offices, because he and his Social Democratic friends see no chance of the SP getting its way with the CP in the new party.' How right he was! And then, noted by Pieck but leaving the sentence ominously suspended in mid-air: 'Boy Ralf, – Nov. 16 years, was supposed to for NKVD – in apartment –'. Yes, that is how it was (or almost, for I was nearly 17 and born in May).

A year after the Nazi Gestapo had collected me from my school near Buckow and interrogated me in its customary way (my father was already under arrest since the coup attempt of 20 July 1944), a similar creature, this time from the Soviet NKVD, came and tried to persuade me during the

20-minute walk home from school, to spy on my father. The second hand of liberty fell, as in my clock, back to its low point.

From Hamburg, to which we escaped, I returned quite often to Berlin in those postwar years, since 1948 as a junior editor of the student-run magazine *Hamburger Akademische Rundschau*. There I published, during the summer of 1948, articles with dramatic headlines: 'What Happened at the University of Berlin? And What Did Not Happen With Us?' This second chain of events which I want to evoke had to do with three students of the Humboldt University, Otto Hess, Joachim Schwarz, and Otto Stolz. I knew the haggard, persistent, clear-sighted Otto Hess best; he was badly scarred by the war but pursued his goals with great courage. His paternal friend, the art historian Carl Georg Heise had dedicated a book about Aby Warburg to him with the poet's pertinent line: 'Blessed he who even then does not rue the fragment of his life.'

Hess, Schwarz and Stolz were editors of the Berlin student paper *Colloquium*. They wrote openly about the attempts by the SED and the Soviet-controlled Administration for Popular Education, to bring the Humboldt University into the party line against the declared wishes of its students. On 18 April 1948 the three were sent down for 'violating the decency and dignity of a student by their journalistic activity'. All appeals remained vain. Most of their fellow-students and almost all teachers went into hiding yet again, too frightened to speak up. Even the support from the West remained modest. American occupation officers and the City Senate under Ernst Reuter were the only ones to take up the case and to support the plan to found a new, Free University in the West of Berlin.

The story is long, and it has been told before. However, one cannot remind the world too often of it. It entails two, if not three important lessons. The first is simply that there are situations in which resistance becomes a civic duty. These are not agreeable situations. Nobody should play them down. Resistance as a leisure pursuit in basically free societies makes actions appear harmless which in more serious circumstances can be a matter of life and death. Hess, Schwarz and Stolz did not play games; they were faced with a relentless regime, like the students of the White Rose in Munich a few years before them.

By not giving in, the three have written a piece of the postwar history of Germany's civil society. It has remained a fairly modest piece, not because of what they did but because of what others did not do. Even if despite threatened sanctions some 2000 of the 12 000 Humboldt students (the police only counted a few hundred) attended a protest meeting, the university as a whole remained as silent as its predecessor in the Nazi period. As a source of civic courage and civil liberties German universities have failed miserably in this century. Even the lack of support for the plan of a Free University makes one wonder. It characterized not only West German universities but also the British occupation authorities – a fact which I register with particular dismay. Moral support for those who risk their civil, and at times their physical, existence in the interest of freedom, is much more important than some may think.

However, the Free University of Berlin did come about. Whatever one may think today about this giant academic supermarket, the foundation of the Free University was an example of effective civil society. Students, as well as frequently unorthodox lecturers, found support with American foundations as well as a courageous City government. They created something new, a university which was in fact not just new but different, with student participation in its administration, also with a strong Faculty of Political Science which took up the tradition of the old School of Politics of Weimar days.

Even the Free University could, however, not bring those back who had been murdered by National Socialist Germany, and it attracted only a few who had managed to escape Nazi terror and were now working in free countries. This is (if the description makes sense here) the third chain of events to which I want to refer. I remember well Gershom Sholem's study in Jerusalem which recalled in every detail the world of the German, the Berlin *Ordinarius*, the full professor of old. Sometimes I meet the physically frail but mentally alert Sir Ernest Gombrich in London. A few days ago, Albert Hirschman celebrated his eightieth birthday in the company of his many friends in Princeton. The list of survivors gets shorter, but the history of German emigration is not forgotten. Its effect both in the host countries and in the inhospitable home country will be felt for a long time to come.

This year has seen the publication of the history of the London School of Economics, which I have written on the occasion of the centenary of the great institution. Few chapters have been more painful to write than that about the years 1933 and 1934. As early as March 1933 the then Director, William Beveridge, and the economist Lionel Robbins met Ludwig von Mises in a Vienna coffee-house. Mises had brought the evening paper with the news that Moritz Bonn, Karl Mannheim, Hermann Kantorowicz and other leading professors had been dismissed from their chairs. The two Britons decided immediately to do something. An Academic Freedom Committee was set up at LSE, and the faculty decided to contribute by paying a voluntary special tax – 1 per cent of the salary for lecturers, 2 per cent for readers, 3 per cent for professors – which would make it possible to receive German emigrants. Soon the LSE initiative was extended to the much larger Academic Assistance Council, later called the Society for the Protection of Science and

Learning. The organizations have helped several thousand emigrants over the years.

The London School of Economics alone benefited immeasurably from the immigration of significant German scholars. There were the labour lawyers of the Weimar Republic: Ernst Fränkel, Franz Neumann, Otto Kahn-Freund, the latter an increasingly influential British jurist. Moritz Bonn came to London for a while, Richard Löwenthal for many years. The criminologist Hermann Mannheim remained at LSE, as did later the sociologist Karl Mannheim. R.R. Kuczynski enlivened demography. Karl Popper arrived at the end of the war, after a long detour by way of New Zealand. Then there was the second generation of those who had left Germany as children or in their teens: Ernest Gellner, Claus Moser, Hilde Himmelweit, John Hajnal, Michael Zander and many others.

This is a score of important social scientists. Natural scientists have not even been mentioned. It is no exaggeration to say that the enormous upswing of scholarship and intellectual life generally in the Anglo-Saxon countries since the 1930s owes much if not everything to immigration from Central Europe. On the other side, that is for the expelling countries under German rule, this self-mutilation meant an irretrievable loss. Germany, and within it Berlin and Frankfurt in particular, may conceivably never again experience those heights of creative intelligence and critical debate which they owed to the mixture of Jewish and non-Jewish ingredients of national culture. Even compared to the brief and all too hectic Weimar years everything has become a little flatter, thinner, poorer. The Weissensee Jewish cemetery, which makes all sensitive visitors pensive and sad, remains a monument to lost times of German history.

But I promised not to spread gloom and doom. Let me then turn to a fourth chain of events which takes us into a very different context and above all further into the theme of civil society; I am referring to the 1960s. Most will associate those years in the first place, and for good reasons, with 1968, the ominous visit by the Shah, Rudi Dutschke, the huge demonstrations, the perplexed authorities, the unlimited hopes of the young which for that reason alone were bound to be disappointed. But the Sixties began earlier, with the '*Spiegel* affair' of 1962 for example, in which Adenauer's government tried unsuccessfully to curb press freedom and which therefore became another proof of the increasing effectiveness of civil society in Germany. Government could not afford to do what it wanted, even at a time at which its majority seemed assured. Then there was the time of Ludwig Erhard's unfortunate years as Federal Chancellor, the first serious dent in the economic growth curve of the miracle country, the rapid expansion of a party of the right, the NPD, which bore unmistakeable traces of the Nazi past, and then the Grand Coalition.

I want to use the essentially harmless recession of the middle of the 1960s for an observation on liberty and prosperity – democracy and economic growth – which may well touch the nerve of the German Question. (Incidentally, you will soon notice that this is not only a German question; it is also, for example, that of post-fascist Spain and post-communist Poland, to mention but two particularly important European countries.) Why did the Weimar Republic end in tears? There are almost too many answers to this question. One of the two intellectual events of postwar Germany was the blossoming of the subject and academic discipline, contemporary history, the beginnings of which were linked with the names of Hans Rothfels and Karl Dietrich Bracher, among others. The other event was Germany's new, and very politically conscious literature, the famous 'Group 47', Heinrich Böll, Günter Grass. The writers would not let go of the subject of Nazi Germany; they above all others have contributed to the much-vaunted 'overcoming of the German past'. Many of the contemporary historians have concentrated, for similar reasons, on the end of the Weimar Republic, a democracy without democrats.

Whatever specific or general causes are put forward for that fateful 30 January 1933, one is probably safe to assume that in public awareness the great depression – unemployment, the fears of the middle class – still provides the prevailing explanation. We know by now that it was in fact not the unemployed who voted Hitler's party, the NSDAP, into power. But (so many believe) just as in a milder form in the middle of the 1960s, the early 1930s gave rise to a mood of anxiety, a search for protection and for strong leadership, in the face of economic threats. If we assume for the moment that this is true: why did the same not happen in Britain, or in the United States where the middle class was if anything hit harder by the Wall Street crash? What is so special about the German connection of economics and politics, prosperity and liberty?

The answer is: precisely this connection is special. Germany is the supreme example of a country in which many saw democracy and economic prosperity as inseparably connected. If one does not work, doubt is cast on the other as well. This applies above all in one direction: if prosperity is in jeopardy, democracy is questioned. Democracy is desirable only as long as it produces prosperity.

This however is a dangerous misunderstanding. There is in fact no causal relationship between democracy and economic growth. To be sure, both are based on the assumption that in a world of uncertainty it is better to rely on the free interplay of autonomous forces (constrained by accepted rules) than to try and plan or direct the world. One may even surmise that democracies are more likely than dictatorships to provide room for markets, and even that market economies will sooner or later give rise to democratic forces. But England was a democracy for a long time without having striking economic growth; the same is true for India. The South East Asian 'dragons' and 'tigers' on the other hand are growth economies without the rule of law or democracy.

Thus economic arguments cannot provide satisfactory reasons or firm anchors for the rule of law and democracy. If one wants to find reasons why the rule of law and democracy are preferable to other constitutional arrangements, one has to argue in terms of protection against dogmatism and tyranny and of the human cost of illiberty. It must be possible to dismiss governments by election, otherwise citizens become subjects. So far as anchoring democracy and the rule of law is concerned, it would be wrong to rely on figures of gross national product and its growth. Democracies are stable where there is a lively, active civil society. In such a condition not everything depends on the state, indeed most things do not. Citizens live primarily in and through associations which they create and sustain themselves. The state adds the rules of public action and gives expression to the desire – the need – for a limited yet effective public sphere. As such it is a state in which civil society thrives, a condition of the rule of law, and of democracy.

The greatest danger to democracy today is that large numbers of people conclude: if the constitution of liberty does not increase our prosperity, then we do not need, more, do not want it. This was one great problem of the Weimar Republic. This is the problem of Spain at the end of the long Gonzales boom. This was the predictable problem of the countries liberated from *nomenklatura* communism. It is to some extent the problem of the new *Länder* in Germany. The most important after-effect of the 1960s may yet come to be seen in the uncontested establishment of civil society in the consciousness of the majority, all the way to the often awkward civic initiatives, to noisy demonstrations, and above all the reduction of the state to appropriate dimensions. Free people do not live by the grace and favour of others, especially not of their political masters. Sometimes they are doing well economically, and sometimes they are not doing so well; but their desire to shape their own lives remains untouched by such conjunctures. To have developed such a sense of freedom, is the real achievement of Germany's postwar history.

But I can hear the sceptics raise their questions. Is all this really true? How does it tally with the unquestioned expectations in the 'nanny' state, or the widespread civil-service mentality? And what is left of liberal values when we get to those who are excluded, asylum seekers, strangers, the poor? Is democracy in Germany really as firmly anchored as my claims suggest? And then: is not all this true only for the West? What about the united Germany as a civil society?

Doubt, even self-doubt, is not unknown to me. Still, I can understand the sceptics' questions. Let me confine myself however to offering a few cautious comments on the last of them, that of Germany united, which is my fifth chain of events.

I belong to those who used to regard German unity as a matter of course in principle, but also as unlikely in reality. I thought so despite my strong and consistent conviction that dictatorships cannot last. Like others, I had not given much thought to the consequences of unity. For example, I am surprised by the near-total rejection of West German media by East Germans, and even more by the fact that here in Berlin the old sector border – the Wall – still seems insuperable for two such excellent newspapers as the *Tagesspiegel* in the West and the *Berliner Zeitung* in the East. Sometimes I find myself comparing the new *Länder* with Ireland, with that rather slow, kind, non-violent country in which there is also (or was until recently) little initiative so that many of the more highly motivated people moved to distant places, to New York and Boston, but at least to Glasgow and Liverpool, in order to return only once they have earned enough money to buy a little house and retirement is imminent.

As you can readily see, I understand little of the historical process which is occurring in Germany and notably in and around Berlin. But my experience as well as my imagination tell me one thing. One cannot simply transfer the history of the old Federal Republic to the new Germany. The results of this history make sense only for those who have themselves shaped and supported the process.

During the last eight years I was chairman of a small foundation which supported publishers, books and journals in the countries of East Central Europe, originally in what turned out to be the final years of communism, then in the early post-communist phase. Thus we began with *samizdat* publications, then sent computers and printers and in the end financed translations, new and often short-lived journals or series of books. In the course of our activity we were struck by how difficult most of the new publishers found it to propose first lists of Western works for translation and publication. Some names kept coming up: George Orwell, Hannah Arendt, Karl Popper. Soon after that a kind of bewilderment set in which could be filled by almost random names, by Derrida and Foucault, but also by Bernanos and Mounier, or by Aron and Berlin. Thus one day we sat down – we, that was Timothy Garton Ash, Leszek Kolakowski, Michael Ignatieff, Brian Magee, Robert

Cassen and I – and played a little game: which hundred books have influenced public discourse in the West since the war above all others?

I do not want to bore you with our discussions about Polanyi and Hayek, about Koestler and Gide, about Adorno and Marcuse, about Burnham and Fourastié, but state only that the little game has made us aware again of the entire world of ideas which determined our Western view of the great forces and trends of our time, but which has of sad necessity bypassed those who were living under communist rule. Such a deficiency cannot be made up after the event. In any case, who are we to tell our neighbours in East Germany and East Central Europe to follow in our footsteps? If this is true even for books, that is for signs of the times which are in principle accessible to everybody, how much more true is it for real history, for example for those chains of events which I have chosen as my subject in this lecture. Even if it could be justified, it would not be possible to appropriate to others one's own history. This is a fact of life which we would do well to accept without reservation.

What then remains? I have moved a long way from that Zero Hour which has brought us here today. Still, it is useful to remember it if only because it shows how far one can move within a relatively short time. I find it difficult to follow the more pompous elements of the current German debate about 1945, notably the misleading alternative of 'liberation' and 'defeat'. You will have gathered from my tale that my own family was liberated and not defeated at the time, but also that others in our neighbourhood had a very different experience of the same events. The common road forward since that time was the key to the German success story. The same may well be true once again after German unification. It makes no sense to try and reinterpret the history which people have experienced for them until they no longer recognize themselves. It does make sense however to seek a common road forward. In this process the experience of Western Germany in developing a civil society will be especially helpful. Freedom is not provided by the state and not by the economy either, but in the end only by our own actions, sometimes against the authorities and sometimes with them, but for the most part entirely without them simply because we are citizens, free citizens in freely chosen associations.

13 Democracy in Germany: an Anglo-German Perspective

This was one of the Weimar Lectures on Germany organized by Bertelsmann Books for an East German audience, and delivered in the Deutsche Nationaltheater in Weimar on 25 February 1996

I feel honoured and pleased that you have come on this Sunday morning to listen to the lecture by someone of whom many of you will never have heard before. Those who know this or that about me may well wonder what this strange bird is about who has come to Weimar today: a British Lord but clearly with a German name, a German professor who for twenty years has been in charge of universities in London and Oxford, a traveller between countries and activities. Let me say a few words about myself then, not for purposes of self-advertisement but for you to know through what spectacles your guest sees his subject: short- or far-sighted? tinged in pink or in shadowy grey? through simple window panes or complex bifocal glasses?

There was a time when I was active in public affairs and thus visible to many. It was in the 1960s. At the time I belonged to those who believed that after the successful reconstruction of West Germany, reform was needed. 'Education is a civil right!' was one of my warcries. Above all I wanted to make sure that German democracy proves itself by a non-violent change of government. (The American political scientist Samuel Huntington has convincingly argued that only countries which have passed the 'two-turnover test' by two constitutional changes of government can be regarded as stable democracies.) The Christian Democratic Union (CDU) seemed set to govern forever after 14 years of Chancellor Adenauer followed by three under Ludwig Erhard. Many of us committed democrats believed that change was necessary. When, at the end of 1966, the Grand Coalition of CDU and Social Democrats (SPD) – Chancellor Kiesinger and Foreign Minister Brandt – was formed, some found this a hopeful sign whereas others feared the total entrenchment of the status quo. In retrospect it is clear that both were right. But the years from 1966 to 1969 became lively and restless and led close to the border of violence, indeed in the end a few steps beyond it. At that time, I joined the only opposition party, the Free Democrats (FDP). I took part in numerous demonstrations and debates as one who wanted change but accepted

135

institutions. The slogan 'Underneath the gowns the dust of a thousand years' meant for me – by contrast to the students who carried the banner – that the gowns had to be cleaned and not abolished.

My 15 minutes of fame, or at least of television notoriety, happened in a sound byte discussion with the humane young revolutionary Rudi Dutschke on the roof of a television recording van outside the civic centre of Freiburg, where the FDP held its party congress at the end of January 1968. We were surrounded by thousands of students and other citizens. Dutschke got excited about the 'idiot experts of politics'. 'There are idiot experts of protest too' I replied with a sudden intuition and thus found the way into the headlines of the tabloids.

I liked Rudi Dutschke and suffered almost bodily when the assassination attempt on him took place a few weeks later. Even then, however, I did not seek revolution but democratic change. For 18 months I campaigned throughout the country. In the September elections of 1969 the seeming miracle happened – by the skin of our teeth, and almost the self-destruction of the FDP, which ended up with 5.8 per cent but knew what it wanted. At least its courageous leader Walter Scheel knew it when he formed, with Willy Brandt, the government of change. 'We have to venture more democracy', Willy Brandt said in his programmatic government statement. He and his foreign minister and those of us who had worked for change, had indeed ventured democracy.

In a minor position, as a deputy foreign minister, I belonged to the new government. But soon, *wanderlust* gripped me and I moved on. The routine of politics, to say nothing of administration, is not my sort of thing. In July 1970 I went to Brussels as a European Commissioner. Since then I have spent less than two years in Germany: four years in Brussels, one year in America, 19 years in Britain. Even before 1960 I had lived important years of my adult life outside Germany, two in England, nearly two in America, and three in the Saarland at a time at which the French franc was the currency and, at least until the referendum of 1955, parties of a 'Europeanized' Saarland separated from Germany had the say.

Some describe me in view of such moves as the 'epitome of a European'. This is not altogether wrong. I have got to know the inner life of Europe pretty thoroughly in a number of places and even worked in the cave of the toothless lion, in Brussels. At the same time it shows little imagination to describe my life as particularly European. After all, I did not move to England in order to spend a few years in another place as a European German, but because I felt at home in the culture of British life and continue to do so. I have never denied my Germanness. Some of my colleagues in the House of Lords attend regular German lessons in which the teacher makes them read articles from German newspapers. Afterwards they will come to me with a grin to demonstrate that they can pronounce (and perhaps even understand) long words like *Währungsunion*, *Kanzlerdemokratie*, and even Helmut Kohl's favourite dish, *Saumagen*. But in the Select Committee on the European Communities of which I am a member, the questions are purely British, such as what the relations between 'ins' and 'outs' will be like if and when monetary union happens and Britain stays outside.

Thus I come to you as someone who carries within him two cultures, and what is more, two very different cultures. From parliamentarism to economic behaviour, to say nothing of historical continuities and discontinuities, no two countries in Europe differ more profoundly than Germany and Britain. The word, Europe, may camouflage these differences, but it does not remove them. In fact, Britain's Europe is in significant respects different from Germany's Europe. Traces of such differences will be unmistakable in these Sunday morning reflections.

Sometimes, in my more sarcastic moments, friends have heard me say that the British have a complicated relationship to their continental partners: 48 per cent like the French but not the Germans, 48 per cent like the Germans but not the French, and 4 per cent do not like either. It is just too bad that an influential and long-serving Prime Minister has given these 4 per cent so much influence. This may not just be sarcasm but it is clearly more than a little unfair. There are after all Britons who like both Germany and France, and above all there are many gradations of likes and dislikes. What is true however is that people on the island are less reluctant than continentals to say that they have never trusted the *frogs*, or that they have always been uneasy about the *krauts*.

Thus there are many shades of attitude towards Germany and the Germans. But one can plausibly describe the dominant image in a few simple statements. Many respect postwar Germany, that is to say the old Federal Republic. They believe that it marks a genuine new beginning, and they have confidence in the success of this venture. At the same time they find the fact of unification – as a reunification – entirely normal. For many Britons it was simply a consequence of historical experience that the division could not last. The costs of the process are widely recognized and accepted. Doubts arise only as second thoughts. The new Germany is after all very big. Some are even more concerned because Germany keeps on describing its national interests as the European interest. Is not monetary union above all a German interest in a European cloak? This is a complicated issue to which I must return. Chancellor Kohl becomes increasingly the symbol of a Germany which confounds itself with Europe. 'Carry on,' some say, 'but leave us out of it; we want to have no truck with it'. 'We must find partners', say the others and encourage the

Prime Minister to try and form an alliance with the Italians, if they do not go a step further and praise French nuclear tests because they hope that the old military alliance may become the core of a new European balance of powers.

These are notions burdened with history, but then the burdens of history are my subject. Chancellor Kohl's linkage, in his Louvain speech, of Europe with war and peace has had a considerable effect in Britain. It is not the effect intended by the Federal Chancellor. 'If Germans start threatening war, things get hot', some say, and it is not always easy to persuade them of what Chancellor Kohl actually meant. In fact his speech did lead into the unfathomable depths of history. These have to do with a question which is far from simple: Why do we want Europe today? Why Europe after the end of the Cold War? And why this particular Europe, the Europe with the capital E and U, the European Union?

The answer given by the Federal Chancellor – which two of his five predecessors, Konrad Adenauer and Helmut Schmidt, have given in similar terms – makes one pause for thought. We need Europe in order to tie in, even tie down, Germany. The rest of my lecture has to do with this peculiar, important, worrying thesis. Tying in Germany – Helmut Schmidt spoke recently of Germany tying itself in, *Selbsteinbindung* – what on earth can that mean?

Germany is not alone in hoping that Europe may have a beneficial effect on internal developments of its members. For example, some years ago Britain's leading financial commentator, Sir Samuel Brittan, argued in the *Financial Times* that Britain could never hope to control inflation by itself. Keynes's notion that a little inflation lubricates the economic engine, runs too deep. The only effective method would be to tie Britain into a European Monetary System. Today we know that this 'tying-in process' did not work; the particular EMS in question has come to rest in more or less peace; and yet inflation has been effectively fought in Britain. Or is there somewhere still the residual hope that inflation remains a more effective means of squeezing the middle classes than all direct instruments to this end?

I also remember conversations about democracy in Spain with Felipe Gonzales before he became Prime Minister. 'I have looked,' he said at that time, 'at a map of international organizations and discovered that the European Communities are the only one among them which never had a non-democratic member. My main task is to secure Spanish democracy. I concluded therefore that I must above all make sure that Spain becomes a member of the EC.' Gonzales was undoubtedly successful in this, though in the end he became a victim of his own success when the 'second turnover', the democratic change of government took place. However, soon after he had become Prime

Minister Felipe Gonzales found that perhaps the EC is too weak to secure Spain's democracy. In stark contrast with his original judgement he decided to concentrate much of his activity on the membership of his country in NATO. With the help of a daring referendum he pushed this through against the prevailing view in his own party. In retrospect he probably regards tying Spain into NATO as the crucial achievement.

These are considerations which – as you will not have failed to notice – have an immediate relevance for the new democracies of East Central Europe. Indeed (to anticipate a conclusion of my argument) I now believe that Polish membership of NATO would constitute a more important safeguard of Polish democracy than membership in a European Union which imposes quotas on the import of Polish mushrooms and raspberries. Poland is the Spain of East Central Europe. It is a large country with its own significant tradition located in a geopolitically crucial position. If there is such a thing as a European interest, Poland must surely be at its core.

However, my concern here is with Germany and with tying it in, or even perhaps down. Europe is supposed to save the Germans from themselves. This is what Konrad Adenauer said many years ago in a private conversation in Luxembourg which was overheard by journalists. This is what Helmut Schmidt says loud and clear and publicly both at home and abroad. This is what Helmut Kohl says now. It would incidentally be worth reflecting on the fact that the other three Federal Chancellors – Erhard, Kiesinger, Brandt, among them above all Brandt – were not known to make similar comments. It is also worth noting that many in Europe share the dark fears of the German Chancellors. This is above all true in France. French foreign policy is incomprehensible without this motive. One hears similar noises in Italy too, and in the Netherlands, and of course in East Central Europe.

The question raised by this sentiment has several facets. The most important of them is whether Germany is in fact endangered or dangerous. Some British Eurosceptics turn the argument round and say that since Germany is no longer threatening, Europe, European integration, becomes superfluous. Another facet is the question whether the European Union is capable even if it tried to tie down its members. During my short time as a minister of state for foreign affairs, the Council of Europe debated the continued membership of a Greece run by colonels.

At the time, early in 1970, it was hard enough to put together a majority for excluding Greece from an organization which administers the European Convention of Human Rights, and I am not at all sure what would have happened if the Greek foreign minister Pipinelis had not volunteered the withdrawal of his country from the Council of Europe before he was asked. International organizations including the EU are better known for their desire to find new members than for their decisiveness in applying their principles. Then there is the question – and this is the facet of the issue of democracy and international organizations which I want to pursue for a few moments – whether in principle external constraints are suitable instruments for bringing about internal stability.

I think they are not. German democracy, and the resulting behaviour of Germany in the world, depends on internal structures, not on external ties. If Germany wants to go astray, no treaty of Rome, Paris or Maastricht will be able to prevent it. That Germany does not go astray, depends on the manner in which it orders its own affairs.

In the middle of those 1960s of which much has been said already, I published a book under the title *Society and Democracy in Germany*. It did not quite become a bestseller, but it sold well and more importantly, it stimulated debates which continue to the present day. Its core thesis was that the German Question is not so much a political question to others as a social question to the Germans themselves, the question of the social conditions for firmly anchoring liberal democracy. This is the crucial question to the present day. Once the internal, social conditions are given, the issue of external guarantees becomes redundant; if on the other hand the internal conditions are lacking, the best external guarantees cannot do the trick. Thus the question is how the internal, social conditions of liberal democracy in Germany are faring.

At the time, in 1965, I was on the whole optimistic, at least so far as Western Germany was concerned. National Socialism (I argued with a thesis which is still controversial among historians) had accomplished the revolution of modernity for Germany. It did so in paradoxical contrast to its traditionalist ideology of 'blood and soil' by in fact uprooting people and destroying inherited institutional structures. Postwar society in Germany began therefore under circumstances which were profoundly different from those of the Weimar Republic. It sought – and found – new answers to four great questions: (1) the creation of effectively equal chances of participation for all citizens; (2) the acceptance of conflicts as a normal, indeed creative element of free societies; (3) the creation of pluralist structures, notably among the leading groups of the country; (4) the spread of public virtues instead of the private virtues of an authoritarian past. My book was far from self-satisfied. In some respects it was in fact a manifesto of radical reform. Yet its basic tone was optimistic. Germany has changed. For the first time in its history its social structures give one cause to believe that democracy rests on stable foundations.

I need hardly re-emphasize that this was a thesis applied to Western Germany. It actually had much to do with the radical reforms of economic structures introduced by Ludwig Erhard. The book contained a chapter on the other response to the German challenges of 1945, East Germany's GDR. The central thesis of this chapter is that the GDR adds 'another negative answer to the earlier answers of history to the question of democracy in Germany', but that it does not have to be unstable if elements of market rationality come to supplement the plan-rational preferences of the regime. Towards the end of the book there are actually a few reflections on the 'probability and the process of reunification'. Big as the differences between the two Germanies are, 'what has grown apart in twenty years can presumably grow together again in twenty years'. Such a development however (thus I argued at the time) will not come from within. If and when political constellations bring about reunification, there remains 'a deep trench of difficulties in the social sphere which are not so easily overcome'. What would be (I asked at the time) the answer of a reunified Germany to the German Question? My cautious conclusion was, 'that the chances of democracy in a reunified Germany which can freely choose its constitution would still be greater than they had been in Germany's past'. A risk remains, but the more securely democracy in Western Germany is founded, the less worrying it is.

Sometimes I am asked how I assess the future of society and democracy in Germany today, indeed whether I would not wish to update the 1965 book to the present. The answer to the latter demand must be no. This is where the 'European' is no longer sufficiently anchored in the structures of his country of origin to be able to claim an in-depth understanding of events. But in this important city in the new and larger Germany, I shall yield to the temptation of making a few comments on the four themes of my book before I return once again to the issue of Germany and Europe.

The *first* theme is the society of citizens in which every man and woman not only has guaranteed basic rights of participation but is also in a position to exercise them. The process of realizing citizenship rights for all is never complete. Moreover it remains forever threatened. Two threats above all are evident today. One is the emergence of a new underclass of the excluded, that is of people who have no access to the labour market or to civil society and its political institutions. These are long-term unemployed but also impoverished single mothers, as well as those who are defined as foreigners even if they have lived in the country for decades, possibly from birth. The other threat is that of a new authoritarianism, the strange longing for civic self-mutilation in an incomprehensible world. Perhaps both themes have a special relevance in the new *Länder* of the united Germany – the first because some feel that they are still denied full citizenship rights, and the second because there is in Eastern Germany as in the other post-communist countries a strange nostalgia, incomprehensible to Westerners, for the homeliness of *nomenklatura* society with its private niches. Both threats are important; but the process of creating equal citizenship rights for all continues apace.

The *second* theme of the social conditions of democracy is the ability to live with conflict. It was never very strongly developed in Germany. Hegel's absolute truths have long remained more attractive to many than Goethe's irony, to say nothing of the enlightened scepticism of Immanuel Kant who reminded us that while we may like to dream of Arcadia, 'nature' compels us, with the help of our 'unsociable sociability' to lead a life of creative antagonisms. In Germany, the preferred method of political decision-making is still the coalition, the alliance, consensus. Others, Anglo-Saxons above all, watch such preferences without envy and believe that they create rigidity and inflexibility. In England one finds at this time a certain *schadenfreude* (the German word has entered English everyday language) concerning the threats to the competitiveness of West Germany's economy and the painful attempts to counter them. Is consensus, is the much-maligned corporatism, the organized cooperation of government, employers and trade unions, capable of achieving this objective? My own attitude to such questions is rather more uncertain than that of my new compatriots who prefer confrontation. French events in recent months do not exactly confirm the uses of confrontation. Still, there is not much of a sense, in Germany, of the dialectics of initiative and control, of open debate within accepted rules, of regulated conflict. As a result both innovation and change are under threat. The future of the economy will have to provide proof that the German method is not one which works only as long as the weather is fine.

Then, *thirdly*, German elites. This is a large as well as a strange subject. Germany's elites have vacillated for a long time between being unduly enamoured with the word, elite, and denying its usefulness altogether. German elites were either too homogeneous, too much a ruling class or even a *nomenklatura*, or they were anxiously trying to tell all and sundry all the time that they had no intention of leading and only wanted to do what their voters, parties and others told them to do. Many confuse democracy with the absence of leadership. There are no places where the leading groups of the future can get to know each other and gather common experiences, no Oxford and Cambridge, no École Normale d'Administration. In fact of course leadership exposed, as it must be, to criticism and control, is the only weapon against what Max Weber called the 'iron cage of bondage' of modern bureaucratic empires. This is not a time of really important leaders; Nelson Mandela apart I could not mention a single name. There are no impressive political classes either; weak leadership coupled with susceptibility for corruption and dishonesty is widespread. Germany is thus not unique. Is it too daring to hope that the move to the capital city of Berlin will improve the state of a diffuse, self-conscious and weak political class?

My *fourth* subject – in the book of 1965 – was the unpolitical German, an apparent preference for what I called private virtues, the lack of civic sense, of a desire for participation, of civil society. This attitude suits the interests of authoritarian regimes. Authoritarianism is different from totalitarianism. Totalitarian regimes are based on the permanent mobilization of all, on uniforms, organized marches, state-controlled organizations for all spheres of life. 'Total mobilization' is often, and perhaps of necessity, the precursor of catastrophes, of war. Authoritarian regimes on the other hand are based on the withdrawal of the subjects to their private world. Whoever does not speak up but works assiduously and beyond that pursues his (or her) more or less edifying inclinations at home, does not disturb the ways of those in power and is therefore left alone. In my view the late GDR was not totalitarian but authoritarian. Today, some dream of the alleged blessings of an Asian authoritarianism as propounded by the Malaysian Prime Minister in his book 'The Asia That Can say No', no to the West of course. Without doubt such tendencies are present in Germany too, where they can connect with a long tradition. However, authoritarianism does not describe German reality today. Civil society is alive and well in Germany, by virtue of the many, often wrongly criticized *Vereine*, the associations and organizations, by civic initiatives of many kinds, and indeed by the critical spirit which is for many associated with the year 1968 of which I have spoken.

What is the upshot of such remarks, which are of course no more than hints requiring more profound analysis? Above all that while there are problems for the social foundations of German democracy these are no greater than those of many other countries. I do not infer from the sketch of an analysis presented here that there are serious internal threats to German democracy. Is that true for the united Germany as well? Are there perhaps particular problems for those who did not have the good fortune to build democracy for forty years, including the two-turnover test, the ups and downs of the economy, 1968 and all that? Certainly, a civil society which sustains democracy has to grow. It has many different forms anyway; even within Germany there have always been several versions. It is therefore not necessary to be overly impressed by particular Western examples. This is not the only problem in the new *Länder*. Institutions imposed from outside must, as it were, be nostrified and appropriated before they can give rise to constructive processes. It would not come as a surprise if anti-democratic tendencies were stronger in the new *Länder* than in the old ones. However while outsiders tend to focus on these particular, painful problems and realize that it will take a generation to master them, there is no good reason to suspect, in the developments of the newer parts of the united Germany, threats to German democracy.

In one respect one might even conclude: on the contrary. In the new *Länder* you have experienced, after the irrevocable rupture of the years 1989–90, an economic shock which the rest of Germany is still to encounter in different form but similar severity. When I wrote my book on Germany in the early 1960s I was not as aware of the complex relationship between economy and society as I am today. I did recognize the radical effects of Erhard's reforms on the social fabric, but I did not yet pose the question why the Great Depression of 1929–32 had produced Fascist or National Socialist movements in many continental European countries but not in England or America where the crisis was no less severe. Today I believe that democracy is stable only when and where it is no longer identified with economic success by its citizens. Democracy makes us free but not necessarily rich. Those who believe that democracy makes them rich will come to doubt its institutions as soon as the first recession comes. This is what is happening today in the post-communist world. It is also an ingredient of the self-destruction of the Weimar Republic.

Our experience throughout the world today is more than that of a recession. Even during a conjunctural upswing structural changes take place which disappoint the deeply entrenched expectations of millions. Along with lifelong employment and a steadily growing secure income, the safety net of the welfare state is in jeopardy. A strong sense of insecurity is spreading. Britain has faced this challenge at an early point. The result is full of new problems; I have been one of those to set on course a public debate on 'Wealth Creation and Social Cohesion'. The country has paid a high price for its competitive economy in the form of low wages, low social transfer payments, a growing underclass, the decay of inner cities and other phenomena of disintegration. Like the United States of America it now has more and more 'working poor', that is people who have jobs but do not earn enough for a decent life. However, no one doubts that these problems can be tackled with democratic means.

Germany, Western Germany, still has to prove that it can cope with the great structural crisis. It has begun to do so, with traumatic effects at Daimler-Benz, Vulkan shipbuilders and others, but the process will continue for years. For the time being, the cuts in social transfer payments are harmless, but these too have only just started. One must hope that Germany will not make the mistake of others and sacrifice social solidarity on the altar of economic competitiveness. But the more difficult question is how this competitiveness can be brought about without people beginning to doubt the uses of democracy. This is the true test of the coming years. Moreover, it is one where West Germans can learn from East Germans, for in the *Länder* of the former GDR and in them alone a profound economic transformation had to be pushed through along with the construction of a democratic state. This was and is a strong test of people's civic sense and their love of freedom. Let us hope that the citizens of Stuttgart and Bremen pass it as well as those of Leipzig and Weimar.

And Europe? The comments, footnotes almost, which I have interspersed in my address on the subject, may well have led some of you to the conclusion that I have ended up not just among the British but among British 'Eurosceptics'. This conclusion would be quite wrong. I may be Euromelancholic, thus sad that this organized Europe seems to lose itself in costly irrelevances rather than tackling burning issues. For me, even monetary union is an irrelevance which detracts from central tasks and splits Europe in the process. The main task today lies in squaring the circle of prosperity, solidarity and liberty. This is where we need each other in Europe. To put together a new European programme to this end – as was begun by the former Commission President Jacques Delors – is worthy of our efforts. It is also the point at which for the speaker to whom you have listened so patiently the several homes, Germany, Britain and Europe, melt into one combined approach to the future.

14 Europe – Unity and Diversity

Keynote Address at the 39th German Historians' Meeting, held in Hanover on 23 September 1992

'In the beginning was Napoleon.' Thus Thomas Nipperdey began his history of Germany in the nineteenth century. How would one begin the history of Europe in the twentieth century? Certainly not with a comparable act of 'creative destruction' (to use Joseph Schumpeter's words). For far too long in this century there was much destruction and little creative construction. One is reminded more of the Cassandra sigh of Britain's Foreign Secretary Sir Edward Grey in those consequential August days of 1914: 'The lamps are going out all over Europe. We shall not see them lit again in our lifetime.' Lamps, not lights were what Sir Edward (soon Lord) Grey talked about, gas lamps, no doubt, as he knew them in Westminster and St James's; they have indeed become victims of technical progress for ever. The same technical progress was soon to cast Europe into quite different and much deeper gloom. From the first tank battles and poison gas attacks and air raids and unlimited submarine warfare right down to Auschwitz and the Gulag Archipelago leads a path of Europe's self-destruction, and worse, the decomposition of its moral texture. In the end we have to ask: does Europe as a civilizing force which gradually finds its political expression, exist at all?

Edward Grey's generation certainly did not see the lamps of Europe lit again. When the long-time Foreign Secretary died in September 1933, the worst phase in the history of the century had only just begun. Those of us who were born later had a better deal, especially if we were fortunate enough to live in the free parts of the world after 1945; in our half of Europe first electric lights, then neon tubes and in the end glaring halogen lamps were lit up. Never before have so many people enjoyed freedom and prosperity in peace for so long as the citizens of the First, the OECD world in the forty years from 1948/49. In the process even something resembling a real, an organized Europe coalesced, with difficulties to be sure, as an Echternach-type procession – one referendum backward, two referenda forward – and always threatened by its internal deficiencies, but in its more auspicious moments almost a European Community on the way towards a European Union. Then the wonderful year 1989 happened in which the lamps began

146

to flicker again in the part of Europe which had been condemned to a miserable life in the darkness of a Soviet hegemony which was sealed in Yalta and confirmed in Helsinki. Poles, Czechs, Slovaks, Hungarians and others with them at last found the path which they believed would take them 'back to Europe'.

But alas! The beautiful days of Warsaw and Budapest, Prague and Leipzig did not last. Today, thoughtful and serious people are wondering whether in this year 1992 the beginnings of a strong united Europe have been buried. They are not just thinking of the Treaties of Maastricht, whose rather minor significance has been exaggerated beyond belief by the exhausted and by now also perplexed gentlemen assembled last December in order to sign them. No, concerned contemporaries are thinking of the Europe of peaceful cooperation of which not much is left in Sarajevo, and of the failure to find common remedies against the quakes of former Yugoslavia and of East and Southeast Europe more generally. They are thinking also of a Europe of openness and of prosperity which does not founder on the cliffs of a recession which some are beginning to call depression, but which out of fear or simply thoughtlessness does little to prevent the erection of a new wall in the East. They are also thinking of course of the Europe of institutions of integration which meets with little support among Europeans, not just in Denmark and in France.

However, sounding the death knell is often a strange mistake, at least in the case of institutions; too many have come to be resuscitated to surprising strength. The least that must be said is that the hourglass of Europe is by no means totally empty. It may no longer be half full, but at least France and Germany have not conducted a war by proxy in Yugoslavia; the 'Europe Agreements' with the new democracies of East Central Europe show some good intentions on the part of the wealthier Europeans; 'Brussels' still exists and the softer breeze of 'subsidiarity' will not blow it away any more than the harsher winds of the French electorate or of Baroness Thatcher and her supporters. There is nevertheless cause to reopen the question: what exactly do we mean when we say, Europe?

Three years before the revolution of 1989, Timothy Garton Ash asked: 'Does Central Europe Exist?' In Warsaw, Prague and Budapest he had been struck by the readiness of people to call themselves Central Europeans. In doing so they had clearly forgotten the old bogeyman, *Mitteleuropa*. They were not thinking of Friedrich Naumann, not even of Germany, but of the simple fact that they no longer wanted to be a part of Eastern Europe. Eastern Europe meant Soviet hegemony, *nomenklatura* rule and grey misery. They sought their place further West. What did they find there? Poles had left the old East European time zone many years ago and counted their hours in

Central European time (which incidentally gave at least their clocks two hours distance from a Moscow which is but an hour-and-a-half away by plane). To the West of the East there is the Centre. Central Europe, so Garton Ash told us, had become for many the epitome of the West.

A few years later this is no longer so certain. In this respect too we see history begin afresh. Germany has become very big in the middle of Europe, and while for the time being it does not derive any claims to hegemony from its size or position, it is no longer unambiguously identified with the West. Poles and Czechs and Hungarians still like to be called East Central Europeans or even Central Europeans, but in the language of their aspirations, 'Europe' has now assumed the place of 'Central Europe'. They have come to speak rather like Spaniards and Portuguese after their transitions in the 1970s. They too had wanted to return to Europe. For Spain this meant the end of a long period of self-imposed isolation, almost a kind of Iberian Meiji revolution. Portugal was faced with an even more difficult task. The country had lived for centuries with its back to Europe and looked out to the vast Atlantic Ocean or at times to the deep South, to Africa. Today both countries – each in its own way – have reconnected with Europe. Thus there must be something that can be called Europe. But what is it?

The initial answer is unavoidably problematic. Europe can be almost an optical delusion. How did Denmark's foreign minister put it after the referendum of 2 June 1992, and with a significant variation of the words which Shakespeare put into the mouth of his Royal countryman? 'To be *and* not to be, that is the question.' Now you see Europe, and now you don't. We are delighted by the diversity of the continent (including, to be sure, the off-shore islands) and the search for unity gives us hope. Is it in the end the peculiar combination of unity and diversity which defines Europe? Is Europe about cultivating diversity while seeking unity? Is there now even a handy political formula for this task, that is the 'Europe of regions' in which 'subsidiarity' keeps the centre at bay?

Alas! such pretty language is not sustained by realities. Whoever speaks of Europe in 1992 has to be more cautious about the harmony of unity and diversity. For today both have turned sour and therefore their combination is all but unpalatable.

Let us begin with the much-praised diversity. 'The dialects raise themselves to the level of literary languages. The provinces strive for autonomy, large cities increasingly refuse to subordinate themselves to the capitals, on the other hand the holders of central office are afraid of particularization. Obscure figures can claim some success with their ethnocentric revolt. Madness begins to titter on Europe's horizon.' This is the still reticent beginning of the worried questions addressed to Europe by György Konrad. He soon proceeds to much more gruesome visions such as the 'ethnically cleansed' regions whose number is in principle infinite. 'Why should there be precisely six autonomous republics in the former Yugoslavia? Why should it not be eight?' Or twenty, one might wish to add. Even in the more acceptable case, they all seek to 'assimilate' their minorities. However, 'we know of simpler methods too. For example, eradicate half the village, spread the news in the other villages, in order to put fear and terror into people in view of the threat of repetition, so that the minority flees head over heels leaving everything behind'. 'Why then are we surprised that even in villages militias are set up which occasionally look more like gangs of robbers?'

This is where the uncritical praise of diversity can take us. It also demonstrates the profound ambivalence of the principle of self-determination. It makes good sense to suggest that people should be able to elect their own governments and even to get rid of them again. However, to stipulate that groups of people have the 'right' to live within certain borders, leads to trouble. Who defines them, the groups as well as the borders? And what happens to those who are different but also live within these borders or right next door? We now know what happens; television shows us the result every day; and those involved experience it in the camps, the cellars, the emergency hospitals of Bosnia, Moldavia, Abchasia. A diversity run wild threatens Europe.

Moreover, this happens at a time at which the unity of Europe has gone astray as well. The contrast between Sunday sermons and everyday reality is no longer bearable. There simply is no path which leads from costly protective measures for breeders of mushrooms or traders of animal feed to European Union. Not even a European Monetary System or Union creates unity among the countries of Europe. All the functionalist tricks from the magician's box of Jean Monnet's disciples in the end contribute to alienating Europeans from the goals of integration, and even from the common exercise of sovereignty in important policy areas.

Thus we experience today a Europe of false diversity as well as false unity. This does not devalue the hopes in a Europe which recognizes its diversity while seeking its unity; but it does mean that we have to rethink and in some respects start again to create its organization. The critical question today is not that of diversity. This is real enough in all its strength and danger. Europe's multifariousness is simply a fact which will not be altered by politicians. Even the cruel homogenization by decades of totalitarianism has not been able to flatten diversity. The critical question today is that of unity. How can we create a Europe which tames the diversity run wild without destroying its creative strength? How must, how should a Europe look which gives its citizens something to hold on to as well as a sense of belonging?

Where does such a Europe begin and where does it end? What determines its agenda both within and without? In short, how can it be defined?

The temptation is great to begin with a geographical 'definition'; but this is also risky. Let me nevertheless yield to it for a few moments. Europe is evidently not the same as the European Union of fifteen. The space defined by the EU is not even economically, let alone politically and culturally relevant. But Europe is not definable by the Organization of Security and Cooperation either. The gigantic space from Vladivostok westward all the way to Vancouver not only has a strangely arbitrary Southern border but above all includes powers which, despite their European past, have long gone their own different ways. Thus Europe is larger than the EU and smaller than the OSCE.

Perhaps one should leave it at that. Or is there a more precise definition after all? It is striking that the great faultlines which give rise to violence occur at characteristic points: at the borders of the Habsburg and the Ottoman Empires, at those of the old Russian Empire, in North Africa, thus wherever Orthodoxy and Islam border on Europe. Bosnia-Hercegowina was a late Habsburg conquest, and a costly mistake as everyone knows by now. And Greece? Does it owe its European reputation in the end more to a schoolboy romanticism informed by Winckelmann and by Byron than to the last millennium-and-a-half of history? It would clearly be easier in a European Union without Greece to find answers to the Turkish question and the problem of Cyprus, to say nothing of Macedonia. Were it not for the fact that Europe has always been strong by its mixtures, one might be tempted to draw its boundary where the Latin tradition ends.

This however is no longer a geographical concept. The idea of a Latin Europe has another, deeper meaning. Michael Stolleis has found words for it in a contribution to the debate about Europe which has recently – late but not too late – begun in Germany. Stolleis strongly recommends what he calls the 'Latin solution' which he defines as a legal historian:

> All notions with which West European legal systems operate today – the majority principle, parliamentary procedures, the fundamental idea that those affected by something have to be able to decide about it, popular sovereignty, the concept of law, the regulation of power by a constitution, the separation of powers, the independence of the judiciary – all this has its roots in the Middle Ages and early modern times, and it is the common European heritage.

The institutions of the republic understood as *res publica*, and in this powerful sense the rule of law – this is not a bad, it is even an operational definition of Europe. I adopt it without reservation. And yet something is still missing. In the end the Latin Europe may be as insufficient as the Cartesian Europe of Jean Monnet. What is missing is the effective force of civic virtues, the deep culture of citizenship. What is missing is that element which widens the Latin into the Western. Europe makes sense if we comprehend it as specifically Western, and that inevitably includes civil society.

'The West' – that is enlightenment, parliamentarism, liberalism, the acceptance of economic development; 'the West' means conversely the renunciation of romantic longing, of deprecatory confrontations not just of 'culture' and 'nature' but also of 'culture' and 'civilization', and of the search for the one and only moral ideal in the complex doings of civil society.

I must ask your indulgence for having quoted myself. There was in this case a special reason, for the quotation is from my 1963 Preface to the German translation of Fritz Stern's *Politics of Cultural Despair*. In other words, it takes us back to the beginnings of the debate on Germany's *Sonderweg*, its peculiar and separate path to modernity. Fritz Stern emphasized in his early book, and many times since, that the elements of cultural pessimism, the critique of civilization, a craze for the natural, and social romanticism were and are present everywhere; what matters is the explosiveness, or otherwise, of their mix. Even Hegel did not remain confined to Germany; by way of T.H. Green he has paved the way for a cloudy collectivist streak in English liberalism, and by way of Alexandre Kojève he has taken historicism all the way to the present-day State Department of the United States. And yet the question of the relationship to the West is nowhere posed as dramatically as in Germany. Poland and the Czech lands are more unambiguously Western than Central Europe.

The dilemma is clearly in evidence if we look at Germany's European policy since 1945. For Konrad Adenauer the integration of Germany into Europe was a part of his insistent effort to bring the wavering country into a West which for him was defined entirely in Latin if not in Roman Catholic terms. Social Democrats and Free Democrats never tired of reminding him that in doing so he represented only one-half of the country; not just the East but Protestantism too was sold short; they voted against the Treaties of Paris and Rome. After that, all German controversies went to rest in the four-poster bed of economic growth and increasing prosperity. In no other European country was there as little interest in Europe in the 1960s and 1970s as in the Federal Republic; one went along with things and paid up and beyond that one played the 'have-it-both-ways' game misleadingly called foreign policy, in which there is nothing more important than German–French friendship and also nothing more important than German–American partnership. The bathos of great declarations in Reims cathedral was invariably followed by the flight to Washington in order to affirm true allegiance to the Atlantic alliance. Then, unexpectedly, German unification, and soon after the project of Maastricht happened. The stunned left sought a new Jerusalem beyond the nation-state and discovered for itself, just for itself, a wholly irreal Europe. Many others, not just on the extreme right, began to wonder whether the Deutschmark is not too important to allow it to disappear in the Ecu. For a while, even more thoughtful minds sought consolation in the thesis that there is no German interest which is not also European. However they soon discovered that others misread this as a claim to hegemony, as an attempt to force German interests on others by giving them a European cloak, and moreover that the thesis is not true. Every European country, even the smallest, has national interests as well; the search for the European overlap is difficult and burdened by imponderables. All of a sudden Europe becomes the great embarrassment for Germany, not just in practical politics but also in those dimensions which are our subject here. How Western is this united German really?

In one crucial respect the thread of this argument is still suspended in mid-air. It may well be that Latin legal institutions and Western civil society are a 'common European heritage'. But does it follow that there must be something like a European Union? Does the unity of deep culture require a unified political form? Hagen Schulze demands a more decisive debate about the new Europe. 'Long live the dispute about the real, the emerging Europe.' But he also reminds us of other, less academic antagonisms which in the past have brought about integration, of 'the fear of communism and appeasement of the West's hegemonial power', and a hundred years earlier, 'the policy of the Prussian government which in its struggle with Austria for hegemony in Germany realized first the economic unification of Central Europe into a customs union and then its political unification into the German Empire'. Against whom is the 'real Europe' supposed to be created today?

Not against the United States or Japan, much as the world of three blocs raises hopes of new protective walls among entrepreneurs fearful of competition and workers worried about their jobs. The resulting world would be one which threatens both prosperity and peace. Moreover one must hope that we are not going to build Europe against a presumed new Islamic or old Russian threat. The hope which occasionally shines through, even with German political leaders past and present, that Europe might serve to domesticate the evil Germans is similarly absurd. Such devious and often half-concealed motives must in the end destroy all sensible plans. But if the evil 'federator' does not exist, there remains only one other, much weaker motive for Europe. Legal institutions and civil society – the Latin and the Western tradition – are not suspended in mid-air. They gain reality only in the framework of the state; and the heterogeneous nation-state has provided such a framework in an exemplary manner. This nation-state is probably the contribution of the nineteenth century to the 'common European heritage'. In it, diverse ethnic, cultural, religious groups find a common basis for enhancing their life chances. It alone guarantees civil rights and the opportunities of citizenship. Raymond Aron is but one witness among many for the vital importance of the nation-state: 'The Jews of my generation will not forget how fragile human rights become once they no longer correspond to citizenship rights.'

Aron wrote this in 1974 in a paper on the question 'Is multinational citizenship possible?' in which he concluded: 'There are no such creatures as "European citizens".' Aron is right; we dismantle the nation-state at our peril unless we put something better in its place first. Aron is wrong too; for the consistent Latin and Western person the heterogeneous nation-state cannot be the last word of the progress of civilization. The nation-state is by its very nature exclusive; it draws boundaries. The rule of law and civic sense, however, are invariably an advance on that 'Idea for a Universal History With Cosmopolitan Intent', in the context of which Immanuel Kant has placed them. The Europe sketched here should be one step forward on the path to a world civil society.

This sounds highfalutin and far removed from reality. It is not intended to detract from the more tangible interests in cooperation. In any case, Kant had no truck with Utopia. He always remained critical and wondered therefore how one would have to think and act if one wanted to achieve certain objectives. He sought yardsticks, and criteria. The argument suggested here will similarly lead to quite practical conclusions. There is much to be said for Europe's nation-states to tackle certain issues together. If and when they do this however, they should be guided by the principles which define the nation-state of Latin and Western description. From such notions a new Europe follows, one that is different from earlier approaches.

Firstly. We need a Europe of lean institutions, not a European superstate, nor an artful Europe of regions. There are good reasons why many in the new democracies of East Central Europe remember the Habsburg days with nostalgia, and some even dream of the Holy Roman Empire (though they are inclined to leave out the German Nation which used to be a part of the concept). In both cases, reality was not quite as appealing as the warm glow of memory; but both were attempts to exercise certain functions of government centrally and at the same time allow a colourful diversity to thrive which is neither organized nor suppressed by the centre. This is indeed a model for Europe.

Following this model, there is need to be cautious with regard to the concept of federalism. It is liable to be misunderstood in two contradictory ways. In Anglo-Saxon usage federalism means centralism; the *Federalist Papers* were written in order to provide reasons for the necessity of a central government in America. Self-appointed 'European Federalists' think along similar lines; they dream of a superpower called Europe. It is hard to see a reasonable argument for such a construction. In German usage on the other hand federalism refers to decentralization. One thinks of Bavaria and of the *Länder* generally, which are all rather artificial entities and cannot do much harm. However, such artificial regions soon lead one further to regions of a more tribal nature, and on to the diversity run wild of which I have spoken. A Europe of lean institutions will only affect the existing nation-states, and also their more or less autonomous regions, as well as local government, cultural communities and religious denominations, at those few points at which the burden of proof for common action is overwhelming. Thus such a Europe will have a structure *sui generis* and defy comparisons with either historical or contemporary political entities.

Secondly. This structure will certainly involve a framework of rules for the economy; thus conditions which encourage economic actors. 'Internal market' is a strange, indeed on closer inspection an illiberal concept, for all markets strain towards openness, and thus the removal of boundaries between the internal and the external. Insofar as Europe's internal market works towards this end, it is desirable; wherever it is intended to be protectionist, it will lead to bloated bureaucracies, costly and probably unsuccessful attempts at redistribution and disturbing interferences in world markets. This is true also for a monetary union, which is conceived primarily in political terms. It makes good sense to aim at creating economic conditions which facilitate the step towards fixed parities and in the end lead to a common currency by market forces. On the other hand, to dictate a calendar for monetary union on the strength of an allegedly powerful political will, must inevitably lead to those deep divisions which 'Maastricht' has brought about in Europe. There were always bound to be those who want to but cannot, those who can but do not want to, those who neither can nor want to, and those who both can and (perhaps) want to. Such incompatible attitudes could easily have been had without any great European efforts.

Thirdly. Under these circumstances it is critical that Europe takes its Latin and Western vocation seriously. An ELU or European Legal Union has much greater priority than an EMU, a European Monetary Union. Europe must embody, cultivate and guarantee the rule of law and democracy;

otherwise it is not worth the effort. If one measures the real Europe on Michael Stolleis's yardstick of the 'common European heritage' – majority principle, parliamentary procedures, popular sovereignty, separation of powers, and so on – the result is pathetic. Perhaps a little caution is in place with the invocation of a 'Europe of citizens'; the lean institutions of a European Union are not supposed to interfere with the everyday world of civil society; we could happily be spared such superfluities as EU tennis tournaments or an EU youth orchestra. But Europe has to become a space for the effective guarantee of civil rights and thereby accomplish precisely that which Raymond Aron did not yet expect from it twenty years ago. European unity, as it is understood here, makes sense only if it develops on a continent-wide level the best traits of the heterogeneous nation-state. Not tennis tournaments but guaranteed basic rights create a convincing Europe of citizens. Speaking of an ELU was not meant frivolously. In this respect the Council of Europe has provided, by the Convention of Human Rights and the Court to go with it, more important beginnings than the European Community. Europe must give its citizens the chance to be proud of belonging to it, and this will be the case only if and when its institutions secure civil rights better and for more people than any other political space.

Fourthly. Clearly all this has something to do with Europe's attitude to the outside world. Two things need to be said on this subject which are at least in theory simple. One is that the construction outlined here would create a European space in which domestic and foreign policy blend into each other at important points. This is a space which creates for its inhabitants the security and perhaps the beneficial constraints to hold them back from the temptations of illiberty. Not the least reason for Spain's desire to join the EC was that it hoped to secure in this way additional guarantees against authoritarian risks. For the same reason, the early membership of the new democracies of East Central Europe in all institutions of European integration is important. Democracy and the rule of law are forever precarious; their common defence provides protection for all.

The other simple conclusion from this argument is that in crucial respects Europe is but one step on the long road to a world civil society. Europe alone is in any case not enough. In practical terms this means above all that Europe must remain a driving force when it comes to establishing worldwide rules and institutions. It betrays its vocation to the extent to which it closes its borders, and in the worst case, tries to keep people, as well as goods from abroad, outside.

Is this all? Is it enough? Does it help to light the lamps all over Europe again? One cannot help thinking of Yugoslavia, and also of Czechoslovakia. One fell apart in a bloody war, the other was separated with velvet gloves;

but both are defeats for the idea which guides a civilized Europe. This idea is the precise opposite of the nightmare of 'ethnic cleansing'; it is the idea of a commonwealth in which, thanks to common citizenship rights, diverse groups can determine their governments themselves, without having to worry unduly about their identity as groups and their borders. It was not wrong that many Europeans initially wanted Yugoslavia, as well as Czechoslovakia, to remain united. I have had few good things to say about the Treaties of Maastricht and the 'functionalist' Europe of the EU; but if reasoned criticism of the reality of Brussels is used to justify a new virulent nationalism, the danger becomes clear and present. The way back to the tribes threatens all of us in Europe. Reversing it is the first task of our time. Karl Popper remains topical:

> The more we try to return to the heroic age of tribalism, the more surely do we arrive at the Inquisition, at the Secret Police, and at a romanticized gangsterism ... We can return to the beasts. But if we wish to remain human, then there is only one way, the way into the open society.

15 From Europe to EUrope: a Story of Hope, Trial and Error

15th Annual Paul Henri Spaak Lecture, given at the Center for International Affairs, Harvard University, on 2 October 1996

Twice in little more than half a century – thus in my own living memory – Europe emerged from the grip of dark forces of evil to the light of freedom. Hitler's barbaric onslaught on liberty and civility led through the hell of the holocaust to a European continent in ruins, in which despite everything the values so savagely attacked had prevailed. That was the challenge of 1945. Then, barely three years later, a large part of Europe was cut off from the new opportunities and enveloped in the brutal denial of rights and life chances by Stalin's tyranny, which later turned into the grey oppressiveness of 'really existing socialism'. But this too did not last. In 1980, *solidarnosc* took up the torch lit and quenched in Berlin in 1953, in Budapest in 1956, and in Prague in 1968. This time, the dictators were in retreat, until finally they had to let go of hitherto communist Europe and leave it in the hands of 'dissident' believers in democracy and the rule of law. That was the challenge of 1989.

I was sixteen in 1945, and had survived a spell in prison and in a Gestapo camp where anti-Nazi activity at school had landed me. Back in Berlin, we were now anxiously waiting for my father to come home from the horrors of camps and, after his trial before the notorious *Volksgerichtshof*, the more orderly cruelty of Brandenburg prison. When he came, he had already been appointed head of energy supplies for the devastated city of Berlin. From his prison days he brought with him the legacy of his Social Democrat friends who had not survived. It was a legacy of unity: unity of the labour movement to prevent a repetition of the political fratricide of the early 1930s which in his view had helped the Nazis to power, and unity of Europe whose divisions had caused two great wars in our own century and several others involving first Prussia then Germany in the century before. Both hopes of my father's were to be disappointed, at least initially and in the way in which they were conceived, before they eventually came to fruition after all in unexpected ways.

The unity of the labour movement met with resistance by the Communists whose leaders had returned to Berlin from Moscow believing that they could go it alone. When they discovered how little support they had for their line of action, they began to force their plans upon the Social Democrats. This my father resisted in turn (as he always resisted force) until in the end he had to leave Berlin in a hurry, saved from Stalin's NKVD by British friends who flew him (and me) out to return to his native Hamburg. A decade later – by then my father had died an early death of exhaustion – it emerged that a revitalized Social Democratic Party did in fact provide that unity which the resistance fighters had dreamt of, for there was no other party of social reform left to command the allegiance of voters.

However, in the early years, postwar Germany's Social Democrats did not support European integration. In 1952, they voted solidly against the Treaty of Paris which created the European Coal and Steel Community (ECSC). My father was devastated and even considered leaving the party which had been his political home since he was 18, if not earlier. It took a decade for the German SPD to shed its curiously nationalist beginnings and become the party of Willy Brandt and later Helmut Schmidt, which was as European and Atlantic as Konrad Adenauer's CDU.

In fact, few of those who invented Europe – a Europe of freedom and civility – after the war came from the political left. Winston Churchill, the British Conservative, made the memorable speech in Zurich fifty years ago almost to the day in which he called for reconciliation and European union. (His was a union of France and Germany to be sure, with the Benelux countries and Italy involved but Britain, still wrapped in delusions of grandeur, a mere 'sponsor' along with the United States and, perhaps, Soviet Russia.) Those who pursued the idea were for the most part Christian Democrats – Alcide de Gasperi in Italy, Robert Schuman in France, Konrad Adenauer in Germany. They were, to be precise, Catholic politicians. Europe acquired a distinctly Roman flavour, all the way to the Treaty of Rome in 1957 to set up the European Economic Community (EEC), and this ultra-montane quality did not necessarily commend it to more secular parties. Paul-Henri Spaak, one socialist among the founding fathers of postwar Europe (at least in terms of party allegiance) characteristically argued even during the war that Britain was essential for European unity, otherwise Europe 'will be organized without and as I dare predict against England and its dominant force will be, despite the defeat, Germany'.

Not just Belgium, but several smaller countries of Europe have from the beginning played a special part in the process. Luxembourg certainly had more than its share if one thinks of Joseph Bech, the Prime Minister from Mondorf-les-Bains just across the border from Robert Schuman's home in

Lorraine, of his later successor Pierre Werner, the author of the first project of Economic and Monetary Union in 1970, and of two of their successors as Prime Minister, Gaston Thorn and Jacques Santer, who later became Commission Presidents. The Netherlands were from the beginning the most effective, perhaps the only force to combine strong support for European integration with insistence on its openness to the world and on democratic accountability. Joseph Luns – one of the few who could look de Gaulle in the eyes for he was equally tall, and he spoke without fear or favour – was but one of a long line of Dutch Europeans, many of whom emerged either from Dirk Spierenburg's foreign office or from Max Kohnstamm's Monnet Committee. Of the newer members of the European Union, the Irish and perhaps the Portuguese continue this tradition of small-country involvement.

But I must take up the thread of my story: my father's deep unhappiness with the anti-European stance of his party. In 1952, on a visit to Amsterdam, he heard of the SPD vote against the 'Schuman Plan' for an ECSC and wrote an emotional paper full of foreboding. He remembered the time 'when in a German prison, he had his own thoughts about what would be after the end of Hitler Germany'. How can Europe be brought into balance in view of the foreseeable East–West differences? 'He saw this as a great opportunity for democratic socialism – and as an obligation of Germany.' But it would require more than recognition of Germany's collective guilt; what was needed was action, even perhaps 'the internationalization of the Ruhr region' (with its coal mines and steel mills). The Schuman Plan is if anything a modest step in this direction, but it is 'a political step in an economically decisive area which will lead to supranational solutions'. Moreover, it prefigures a future which will attract hitherto passive young people to political involvement. How can Social Democrats, instead of forming the vanguard of this future, defend 'national and other faintheartedness'?

Rereading such exhortations 44 years later, one is struck by how much has changed, not least in the views then held by German Social Democrats – views which are now more likely to be found among British Conservatives. One is also reminded of the question what Europe – 'supranational', or at any rate organized Europe – is about. The answer is by no means obvious. In part (or so I have long thought) it is actually about small countries. Without joining forces with others they would be nowhere in this world of ours, and yet they have so much to offer. Moreover, since the larger European nations are not exactly superpowers, the experience of the smaller ones is relevant even for them. But this is just one motive. Another one undoubtedly has to do with the past. One must be allowed to wonder whether it was actually European integration which has prevented wars at least among the members of Europe's Communities after 1945, though one impetus for cooperation was undoubtedly to put an end to the dismal past.

In practice this meant that Europe since 1945 was always about Germany, Germany as an acceptable partner, a Germany that is contained by inclusion. One cannot but admire the sentiments Churchill expressed in Zurich in 1946: Germany's crimes (he said) are not forgotten. 'The guilty must be punished. Germany must be deprived of the power to rearm and make another aggressive war.' But then 'there must be an end to retribution'. 'There must be what Mr Gladstone many years ago called "a blessed act of oblivion".' And then the famous passage: 'I am now going to say something that will astonish you. The first step in the re-creation of the European Family must be a partnership between France and Germany. In this way only can France recover the moral and cultural leadership of Europe. There can be no revival of Europe without a spiritually great France and a spiritually great Germany.'

Thus, let us remember, on 19 September 1946, a mere 16 months after Germany's total defeat! It did not quite happen that way, of course. Not only is Britain hardly the 'sponsor' of this Franco–German Europe, but France is far from being its moral and cultural leader. Only the apparent need to 'tie in' Germany has remained, *a fortiori* after the end of the East–West divide which so conveniently held the Western half of Europe together. Europe for many is about keeping Germany under control, and it is not just French politicians who feel that way. At least three German Chancellors – Adenauer, Schmidt and Kohl – showed a strong sense of the need for Germany's *Selbsteinbindung* (to use Helmut Schmidt's term), that is for the country to tie itself to its European neighbours in order to prevent the recurrence of past aberrations. (The other three Chancellors, incidentally, did not express such views, though each for his own reasons; they were of course Ludwig Erhard, Kurt Georg Kiesinger and Willy Brandt.) All the way to monetary union, one motive force of European integration has remained the desire to keep Germany within the fold.

Within what fold? For one thing, to be sure, the fold of the liberal democracies of the world. Not only was the Second World War fought and won in the name of democracy and the rule of law, but democracy at home is also as solid a guarantee against aggression abroad as one can hope for. As a rule, democracies do not start wars. Clearly, in this regard, the postwar hopes for Germany have been fulfilled, though one may doubt whether the role of European institutions in creating a firm social basis for Germany's democratic political institutions was more than marginal.

There is however another aspect of the fold within which Germany was, and is to be kept, and it is even more relevant after unification than before.

A lingering concern remains whether Germany might not drift off once again to its old Eastern destiny. *Ostpolitik* has heightened this concern, and unification may appear to give it a certain practical plausibility. Yet in this respect too, postwar changes have been remarkably successful. The success lay not so much in persuading Germany and the Germans of the values, institutions and orientations of the West (important though this was) as in a much more fundamental and effective process. The German author Wolf Jobst Siedler called it, perhaps slightly wistfully but no less convincingly for his regrets, the *Westverschiebung Europas*. The term is justly geological; we are talking about a kind of continental drift: Europe itself has shifted to the West. 'Europe regained is a Europe which looks to the West.' The East is gone as an option. 'Europe's East does not want to be an East' in the old, emphatic sense of the Slavophiles. Indeed, where are the Slavophiles now?

Timothy Garton Ash made this point in one of his remarkable *New York Review of Books* pieces years before the revolution of 1989. 'Does Central Europe Exist?' he asked in 1986, and replied: not yet. It was then still an idea, if a potent idea, the antithesis to the Soviet 'imperial system whose main instruments of domination are lies, violence, the atomization of society'. He described the alternative by 'the imperatives of living in truth, nonviolence, the struggle for civil society – and the idea of Central Europe'. We rarely refer to Eastern Europe these days, and when we do we mean the Ukraine and places further east. Actually, they too want to be part of a Europe which is essentially Western in its values and institutions. The decline of the East, or so it appears, is terminal, and Europe's shift to the West irreversible. This, among other consequences, is the answer to the German Question.

It is not however as such the answer to the European Question. Those of us whose dormant liberal passions were reawakened, indeed redoubled by the collapse of *nomenklatura* communism in 1989 and 1990, have since seen some disappointments. Once again, great figures emerged to speak for their newly liberalized countries: Lech Walesa in Warsaw, Vaclav Havel in Prague, Arpad Göncz in Budapest, Zheliu Zhelev in Sofia, and others around them. A new Europe could have been built on their visions, but it was not. Their Western counterparts did not have the stature to live up to the challenge of liberty regained.

The disappointments of those of us in the old Europe who trembled and later rejoiced with our friends in Poland, in Czechoslovakia, in Hungary and elsewhere are thus not the obvious ones. They are not due to the slow progress of the economies and civil societies of post-communist countries which was to be expected and continues to be a challenge to their own citizens as to those of us who are ready to help. Even the valley of tears through which people would have to trek before things got better did not come as a surprise. The key disappointment is the response by us, the more fortunate Europeans, to the needs of those for whom the idea not just of Central Europe but of Europe should now be real. Not to put too fine a point on it, Western Europe has betrayed its principles and promises when instead of stretching out its hands to Central Europe it has turned inward to its own so-called *approfondissement* à la Maastricht and even allowed the protection of ludicrous vested interests – in rationing imports of mushrooms and raspberries from Poland for example – to prevail over political imperatives. Institutionally at least, EUrope – the European Union – has failed Europe, the continent in need of cooperation and integration.

This then takes me from 'hope', one part of the title of this lecture, to the other, 'trial and error', and worse, from reality to the arcane and rather uninspiring world of European institutions. Worse still, here I have to part company with my father who believed that a 'political step in an economically decisive area will lead to supranational solutions'. The company with which I part was, to be sure, distinguished. All the founders believed that the economic beginnings would in the end result in European union. Thus I have to part company with Walter Hallstein, the first President of the EEC Commission, and even with the patron saint of European integration, Jean Monnet.

Churchill's and others' dream first gained institutional reality when the Council of Europe was created in 1948. You may call this a Eurocentric statement for there was after all that other venture, the Organization for European Economic Co-operation (OEEC) initiated here at Harvard with George Marshall's important address on 5 June 1947. The Marshall Plan was the greatest single stimulus to European recovery, but it did not unite Europe. OEEC always kept its Atlantic flavour. This did not detract from its success. Even today, the extended OECD, now an Organization for Economic Co-operation and Development among the rich countries of the world, is an unrivalled source of socio-economic information and co-ordination, but contrary to the Council of Europe, Europeans never regarded it as 'theirs'. Our own Council of Europe was, and is, an intergovernmental – as distinct from a supranational – organization. This may be one of the reasons why it failed to meet the high expectations which accompanied its birth. Its most important purpose today is in the human rights field through the administration of the European Convention, particularly in the new member states in East Central Europe.

However, by the early 1950s it had become clear that other, more effective ways had to be found to bring the free countries of Europe together. The Coal and Steel Community was one such way, more remarkable for its institutional arrangements than for its substance. On substance it is perhaps worth mentioning that a Community founded to establish the joint governance of 'heavy industries' which had given rise to conflicts for a century and more, soon found that it was in fact administering declining industries. One might surmise that this stubborn fact turned the Community from an orientation to the future to one to the past, from a forward- and outward-looking to a protectionist institution – a virus which the European Union has found it hard to shed. To return to institutions however, the ECSC was Jean Monnet's first shot at supranationalism, that is of national parliaments relinquishing sovereignty to a High Authority. It set by the same token an example of how supranationalism makes democracy and even accountability more generally difficult.

However, in the early 1950s, the ECSC was not regarded as the nucleus of a European Union. At that time, more directly political ways were sought, defined and negotiated to the point of treaties. At that time also, France was clearly the driving force, the 'leader' as Churchill had hoped. Rather, French governments played that role, both in the design of a European Defence Community (EDC) and in the proposal to create a Political Authority for a 'European Community of supranational character' fashioned on the ECSC. But Governments had rushed ahead of their peoples. The EDC failed in 1954 in the French parliament, and the plan for political union was quietly dropped as a result. Instead NATO was extended to include Germany, and in Europe the unfortunate process began which is with us to the present day: the process of trying to achieve political objectives by means of economic integration.

The facts are familiar. In 1957 the Treaty of Rome was ratified in the parliaments of six countries: Italy, the Benelux countries, France and Germany (this time with the votes of some though not yet all German Social Democrats). The EEC began its life in 1958, along with the European Atomic Community (Euratom). Ten years later, the ECSC, the EEC and Euratom were merged into the European Communities. In 1973, the first major enlargement of the EC took place with Britain entering the scene. After the turbulent 1970s with the failure of the first project of monetary union, and the successful 1980s in which the Single European Act led to the completion not just of a Common but of a Single Market largely without non-tariff barriers, the Treaty of Maastricht in 1991 mapped out a new programme and involved renaming the creature, European Union (EU). From this time onwards, if not earlier, the European Union went seriously astray.

The reasons lie deeply in the history of the process which I have described here. I hope you will forgive me for tracing them in a somewhat personal manner, not for autobiographical reasons, nor because one person's vexations in the European maze are of particular interest, but to give you a sense of the depth of feeling which Europe, and even more so, EUrope can arouse.

In December 1969, a particularly successful European Summit took place in The Hague. It was here that the French veto against Britain's accession was finally lifted. Major steps towards the deepening of European cooperation were also accepted. I was therefore pleased when, having been a Parliamentary Secretary of State in Willy Brandt's government, I was nominated as one of the German Commissioners of the EC beginning in July 1970. My responsibility for foreign trade and foreign affairs made the move all the more attractive. However, when I arrived in Brussels I knew little about the EC, its organization and culture. In the German Foreign Office it had been regarded as of secondary importance, a fact clearly indicated by the denomination of the most senior official in charge of European affairs not as undersecretary *of* the foreign office (a title reserved for the man in charge of general policy) but merely as undersecretary *in* the foreign office. However, I soon found out what was what, and I did not like it. To be sure, I did like my colleagues, notably the great European Altiero Spinelli, a victim of both Hitler and Stalin yet an inveterate idealist, and the stubborn inventor as well as defender of the Common Agricultural Policy, Sicco Mansholt, and also the shrewd future French Prime Minister Raymond Barre who was then in charge of the project of monetary union. But when it came to the institution itself I soon found myself a sceptic.

In July 1971, a year after my arrival, I could not hold my fire any longer. I published a series of articles, under the pseudonym 'Wieland Europa', in the German weekly *Die Zeit*, entitled 'Beyond Brussels. A Plea for a Second Europe'. They turned out to be a bombshell. The thrust of my argument was simple. We have reached the end of the tether of the original treaties. The contradiction between its political objectives and the daily reality of the European Community has become abundantly evident. The supranational illusions of the European beginnings have turned out to be an obstacle rather than a motive force for real political cooperation. The illogical road to Europe has led us into a *cul-de-sac*: the logic which would force countries to move from a problematic agricultural policy to monetary union, and from economic to political union simply does not exist. All that was garnished, in my articles, with highly quotable – and soon much quoted – phrases like: 'There are situations in which [the Commission] causes pity rather than respect.' Or: 'A democrat must be ashamed to see grown-up parliamentarians enact the farce which they have to play ten times a year in Strasbourg and Luxembourg.'

My pseudonym did not stick for long, and it was disingenuous of me to believe that I could persuade the world to distinguish between the author and the Commissioner Dahrendorf. A Europe-wide outcry nevertheless did not lead to my resignation or removal from office. Parliament had a tense hour about 'Wieland Europa' on 23 September 1971, in which only the Italian Communist member D'Angelosante supported my views. The Commission however was generous. Raymond Barre said that he would not do anything to cast a shadow on Franco–German relations, and Sicco Mansholt remembered that as a young man he had also done silly things. I apologized, and much was forgiven, though perhaps in those days the seeds were sown for my later English incarnation. I was reappointed to the Commission after the 1973 enlargement, but in the autumn of 1974 left Brussels to become Director of the London School of Economics. Since then, I have lived in Britain, now not only a British citizen, but as Lord Dahrendorf of Clare Market in the City of Westminster, a member of the Upper House of Parliament, and of its European Communities Committee on which I have acquired the reputation not of a 'Eurosceptic' but of a 'sceptical European'.

I strongly believe that Europe matters and that Britain must be a part of it. My scepticism is entirely about the path which the process of European integration has taken – its inward-looking bias, its serious lack of democratic accountability, the increasingly unbearable gap between aspirations and realities, and then the fatal flaw of the theory that (to quote Walter Hallstein) 'all politics is a unity', so that starting in one corner of economic policy will lead to a 'chain reaction of integration'.

Monetary union, the centrepiece of the Treaty of Maastricht, illustrates the fallacy. In the early 1970s, the first try failed because Europeans had set their calendar without regard to the rest of the world. When the convertibility of the dollar into gold was suspended in August 1971, a process began which swept away all the well-laid plans of Pierre Werner and Raymond Barre. This may not happen again, though the invisible hand of 'the markets' remains a threat even to the much more sophisticated plans of the late 1990s. But for all their sophistication, these plans have two serious weaknesses: they are irrelevant, and they are divisive. The irrelevance results from the fact that monetary union fails to address what people rightly perceive as the real problems of the day, which are unemployment, and supply-side obstacles to competitiveness. The divisiveness of monetary union has to do with the emergence of 'ins' and 'outs'; even if the latter are, as the jargon now has it, 'pre-ins', an inner core will move ahead, and European Union will for a long time be a two-tier arrangement.

The case for monetary union in Europe is primarily political. Chancellor Kohl certainly thinks of the day on which he overrode the views of all experts and pushed through the theoretically mistaken yet in practice inevitable decision to create German monetary union on the basis of a 1:1 exchange rate between East and West Germany. This feat, he believes, can be repeated in Europe, and lead to instant unification. For France, monetary union means regaining some of the powers which are now lost to the Bundesbank, and of course, tying Germany in. Italy and Spain dream of being in the First Division, and also of eternal stability. Britain, as all others accept, will continue to play cricket while they play soccer. But will political union really be the ineluctable result? Or will the whole plan founder on its political non-viability? Will the convergence criteria of fiscal policy lead to domestic unrest in France and elsewhere? Will there be shocks, asymmetric or otherwise, between the 'irrevocable' decision of 1 January 1999 and the actual implementation of monetary union for citizens in 2002?

It is tempting to interpret the history of postwar Europe as one of political stabilization by economic growth and prosperity. Yet here as elsewhere one must beware of the elementary confusion between correlation and causality. The economic and the political miracles happened at much the same time, but it does not follow that one caused the other. More particularly, economic success did not stabilize democratic institutions, even if people found it easier to accept the constitution of liberty at a time of increasing prosperity. Since 1989 we have learned that if anything the reverse of the Marxian theory of the primacy of economics – a theory now held mainly by capitalists – is true. The economic reforms by Leszek Balcerowicz in his brief but crucial period as Polish minister of finance were very important, but the institutional stability of the Polish state despite changes in government matters as much if not more. Where there is doubt in political institutions, economies do not flourish. The invisible hand cannot replace or create the visible hand, and healthy communities need both, they need functioning markets and reliable rules based on stable institutions.

The relevance of such observations for Europe is clear. If we want political union, no economic subterfuge will get us there. Money, it is true, marks the boundary between politics and economics. The stabilization of the Zloty was itself an institutional accomplishment. Argentina's economics minister Cavallo may well have been right to enshrine the pegging of the peso to the dollar in the constitution of his country. But Poland and Argentina existed before, and would have existed even with highly unstable currencies; Europe does not. The next push for European Union has to be political, not economic. If we want to move forward, we shall have to return to the plans and ideas of the early postwar years. Reading the European Convention of Human Rights into the EU treaties might well give citizens more of a sense of allegiance than any amount of Brussels propaganda for monetary union. Even if there is no case for reviving the European Defence Community as long as NATO serves us well, West European Union (WEU), another relic of the postwar days, deserves a good look and perhaps some link with the projected

Common Foreign and Security Policy. Even the plans for a Political Authority might be revived.

Europe matters. I have recently made the case in a little pamphlet (*Why Europe Matters: A Personal View*) which was intended to set the tone for a new Centre for European Reform in London. The Centre will provide ideas on which governments, and notably a government led by Mr Tony Blair, might wish to draw. It defines Europe as a matter of the head rather than the heart, and it aims at closing the gap between realities and aspirations. It does so in a constructive spirit, and in the hope of changing the tone of the British debate, which has become absurdly emotional.

In the year before Britain's entry into the EC, the political economist Andrew Shonfield was invited to give the prestigious BBC Reith Lectures. He spoke about Europe, of course. At the time he introduced a notion which in retrospect sums up the achievements of European integration better than any catalogue of directives and regulations, the notion of the 'habit of cooperation'. Europe has to develop this habit to become real, Shonfield argued. In fact, Europe has done so. Politicians, civil servants and alas! lobbyists have long discovered Europe as their preferred playground. But the habit of cooperation extends much further. Students, young people generally, move easily across European cultural borders. Professionals consult naturally with their colleagues elsewhere. On the boards of foundations and charities, of non-governmental organizations of all kinds the question is asked: what are our European partners doing? Traces of a European civil society are thus unmistakable, even if media and political parties and much else remain national.

Extending the blessings of this habit to the new democracies of East Central Europe is the next major task. It cannot be said too often: widening is deepening because it expresses a common interest of those who are already 'in'. EUrope has to become Europe if it is not to fail its mission.

Where is all this supposed to lead? I have spoken of trial and error not in a critical vein but to indicate that the purposes of the European process are fundamentally open. Andrew Shonfield gave his Reith Lectures the title *Europe – Journey to an Unknown Destination*, which sums up my intentions too. The entire debate about federalism and *Europe des patries* and the United States of Europe and the Brussels Leviathan, and even about European Union is pointless. We do not know where European cooperation will end, but we can take the next steps in response to real challenges and expect an 'ever closer union' to result.

We do know, however, what is not intended. It is two things. For one, there is no point in Europe trying to opt out of the global marketplace, or of attempts to create universal political institutions. Protectionism and parochialism would be the end of a Europe that matters in the world. Once again let me quote from Winston Churchill's 1946 Zurich speech, which has put the case so well:

> There is no reason why a regional organization of Europe should in any way conflict with the world organization of the United Nations. On the contrary, I believe that the larger synthesis will only survive if it is founded upon coherent natural groupings ... They do not weaken, on the contrary they strengthen the world organization. They are in fact its main support. And why should there not be a European group which could give a sense of enlarged patriotism and common citizenship to the distracted peoples of this turbulent and mighty continent?

The forces of globalization are so strong that perhaps the dangers of regional blocs should not be overrated. In any case, insofar as they exist at all they come from regions of another kind (which present the second undesirable perspective). The new world of global information and of the resulting financial and other markets is an uncomfortably exposed place for many. People seek shelter, and they seek it in smaller, allegedly homogeneous units. Far from wanting to be world citizens, or even Europeans, they feel that Italy is too big and diffuse for them and prefer Padania. They prefer the Czech Republic to Czechoslovakia, Wallonia to Belgium, Catalonia to Spain. The search for such mini-nations is understandable in a homeless world; yet it is also dangerous. It is an invitation to warlords and demagogues. It can lead to intolerance within, given that there are always minorities which do not 'belong'; it can also lead to aggressiveness without, given that boundaries are precarious and the closest neighbours are usually perceived as the greatest threat. In such conditions Europe has a new, important mission. It is the balance of sanity for destructive desires. If it gets its act together and abandons reckless plans which must lead to new divisions, a Europe of trial and error can even become a hope for liberty in turbulent times.

Acknowledgements

Chapter 1

Must Revolutions Fail? Unpublished manuscript.

Chapter 2

The Open Society and Its Fears. Original German: 'Die offene Gesellschaft und ihre Ängste'. Published in Verhandlungen des 25. Deutschen Soziologentages: *Die Modernisierung moderner Gesellschaften*, ed. W. Zapf. (Campus: Frankfurt 1991).

Chapter 3

Citizens in Search of Meaning. Unpublished manuscript.

Chapter 4

The Good Society. Published by The London School of Economics in 'The 1949 Seminar Memorial Lecture Series', 1993.

Chapter 5

Morality, Institutions, and Civil Society. Published by the Fondazione Giovanni Agnelli, Torino 1992. (Simultaneously in Italian.)

Chapter 6

Why Excellence Matters. Published by the Fondation Latsis Internationale, no. 3, Geneva 1995.

Chapter 7

Prosperity, Civility and Liberty: Can We Square the Circle? Published in *Proceedings of the British Academy,* vol. 90, '1995 Lectures and Memoirs', London 1996.

Chapter 8

The Democratic Revolution, or The Uses of the Science of Politics. Published by the University of Bologna and the Community of Forlì, 1991. (Simultaneously in Italian.)

Chapter 9

Who Makes History? On the Entanglements of Economics and Politics. Unpublished manuscript.

Chapter 10

Whither Social Sciences? Published by the Economic and Social Research Council, London 1995.

Chapter 11

The Public Responsibility of Intellectuals: Against the New Fear of the Enlightenment. Unpublished manuscript.

Chapter 12

Berlin For Example: From Zero Hour to Civil Society. Original text German: '50 Jahre Frieden in Deutschland: Neu Beginnen, oder Anläufe zur Bürgergesellschaft'. Unpublished manuscript.

Chapter 13

Democracy in Germany: An Anglo-German Perspective. Original text German, published in 'Weimarer Reden über Deutschland' by Bertelsmann Buch AG and Stadt Weimar, 1996.

Chapter 14

Europe – Unity and Diversity. Original text German: ' Europa – Einheit und Vielfalt'. Unpublished manuscript.

Chapter 15

From Europe to EUrope: A Story of Hope, Trial and Error. Published by The President and Fellows of Harvard College, November 1996.

Index

Index by Auriol Griffith-Jones